Between Real and Unreal

Studies on Themes and Motifs in Literature

Horst S. Daemmrich
General Editor

Vol. 49

PETER LANG
New York • Washington, D.C./Baltimore • Boston • Bern
Frankfurt am Main • Berlin • Brussels • Vienna • Oxford

Stefan Bergström

Between Real and Unreal

A Thematic Study
of E. T. A. Hoffmann's
"Die Serapionsbrüder"

PETER LANG
New York • Washington, D.C./Baltimore • Boston • Bern
Frankfurt am Main • Berlin • Brussels • Vienna • Oxford

Library of Congress Cataloging-in-Publication Data

Bergström, Stefan.
Between real and unreal: a thematic study
of E. T. A. Hoffmann's "Die Serapionsbrüder" / Stefan Bergström.
p. cm. — (Studies on themes and motifs in literature; vol. 49)
Includes bibliographical references.
1. Hoffmann, E. T. A. (Ernst Theodor Amadeus), 1776–1822. Serapions-Brüder.
2. Fantastic, The, in literature. I. Title. II. Series.
PT2360.S5B47   833'.6—dc21   98-30525
ISBN 0-8204-4275-5
ISSN 1056-3970

Die Deutsche Bibliothek-CIP-Einheitsaufnahme

Bergström, Stefan:
Between real and unreal: a thematic study
of E. T. A. Hoffmann's "Die Serapionsbrüder" / Stefan Bergström.
–New York; Washington, D.C./Baltimore; Boston; Bern;
Frankfurt am Main; Berlin; Brussels; Vienna; Oxford: Lang.
(Studies on themes and motifs in literature; Vol. 49)
ISBN 0-8204-4275-5

The paper in this book meets the guidelines for permanence and durability
of the Committee on Production Guidelines for Book Longevity
of the Council of Library Resources.

© 2000 Peter Lang Publishing, Inc., New York

Printed in the United States of America

Table of Contents

Introduction

General Introduction

This is a theme-oriented study which focuses on E.T.A. Hoffmann's comprehensive short story collection *Die Serapionsbrüder*. The title *Dark Mirrors: Elements of the Fantastic in E.T.A. Hoffmann's "Die Serapionsbrüder"* reflects the dualistic contrast between the worlds of everyday reality and a supernatural sphere (the latter often having a somber character) in the author's production. The primary purpose of the project is to closely examine the themes of supernatural forces and uncanny events in this writer's works of fiction, mainly as they are reflected in the collection *Die Serapionsbrüder*.

The sparse previous studies on this collection of short stories (at least those considering the work as a whole) have often focused on the narrative structure of the individual tales as well as on structural aspects of the work in its entirety. Recent scholarship has also approached the connection with contemporary communication theory. Moreover, modern research has also addressed questions such as the compatibility of the stories with the general framework of the collection, the varying narrator perspectives, the role of the dialogues, the nature of the "Serapion Society" etc.

This study will take the above mentioned more technical aspects of the stories into consideration only to the extent to which they play a significant part in an analysis of the examined main (and possible related) themes. But this new presentation will emphasize the thematic content rather than the structural form of the chosen work.

The theoretical approach to the occurrence of the fantastic in literature as Tzvetan Todorov has presented it will be of particular significance for my research. Especially Todorov's distinction between the "pure" fantastic, the "uncanny" and the "marvelous" will be valuable in this regard. An introductory chapter will discuss Todorov's ideas in detail and also present more recent criticism of this scholar's approach to the phenomenon of the fantastic in literature. The introductory chapter will also address the issue concerning how this theoretical system fits into an analysis of Hoffmann's production as well as the problem regarding how this system might have to be modified for this particular purpose.

This study also aspires to demonstrate that there is a unifying theme in most tales included in *Die Serapionsbrüder*. This theme is the occurrence of the fantastic as a primary driving force of the narration. An analysis of this topic will have to discuss in great detail the nature of the fantastic elements and how they affect the characters of these narratives. Todorov's structuralist approach to such features would form the most essential (but by no means exclusive) basis for the analysis.

The study also addresses the question as to whether or not supernatural power is limitless or in any way containable.

Several previous attempts have been made to analyze Hoffmann from the point of view of a single major theme. Such attempts have often produced very valuable and interesting scholarship. The appraisal of the author's work in terms of modern psychology for example, has unquestionably led to great progress in the understanding of his works. An emphasis on special aspects of a psychological interpretation, such as sexual psychology, as exemplified by James McGlathery's fascinating *Mysticism and Sexuality: E.T.A. Hoffmann*, have provided indispensable new insight into Hoffmann's creative process. This project will give such psychological approaches some necessary attention.

After having given these earlier efforts some well-earned credit, it should be noted, however, that the author of this study does not agree with some of these psychological interpretations of the fantastic elements in Hoffmann's production. There is always danger of falling into the trap of "psychological reductionism." The aspiration of this project is to avoid such a pitfall. This study rejects the notion that all fantastic components included in Hoffmann's tales only exist in the heads of some of the characters in the story. The presupposition of the project will, on the contrary, be that many of the fantastic occurrences in the accounts actually do take place and that the supernatural phenomena appearing in the narratives in fact have an objective existence within the framework of such a text and outside the minds of the characters involved, and that this is an issue completely separate from the question regarding whether the author himself really believed in supernatural phenomena or not.

The basic analytical model chosen for this study (Todorov's theoretical framework) will also provide the foundation for the choices of material analyzed. Todorov (as do some other literary theorists) makes a clear distinction between the fantastic and fantasy. The concept of the fantastic is based on the notion of "hesitation" when the reader or a character in a story faces a supernatural event. The issue for the reader is whether or not such an occurrence really takes place in the narrative. Fantasy on the other hand simply accepts the supernatural as a part of its own inner reality without questioning it. A typical fairy-tale thus exemplifies fantasy but not necessarily the fantastic. It is true that such stories correspond to Todorov's definition of the "pure" marvelous, but they nevertheless are quite separate from this scholar's main point of interest. For this reason, the decision has been made to exclude accounts that Hoffmann himself refers to directly as "Märchen" from a close investigation in this study. The project will nonetheless briefly touch upon those stories (including "Nußknacker und Mausekönig" and "Die Köningsbraut") when they parallel in some way other tales in the collection. Scholars have already paid a substantial amount of attention to these stories. The same could undoubtedly be said for some of the narratives more extensively discussed in this study ("Die Bergwerke zu Falun" is one example), but those accounts fit much better into a discussion of the nature of the fantastic, and especially into the main framework which has been chosen for this project.

The study will ultimately tie the various aspects of the fantastic in Hoffmann's works together in a comprehensive discussion of the author's treatment of the concept as a whole. In order to broaden the context of the study, the project will compare the author's approach to this theme to his depiction of the fantastic elements (including supernatural forces) in general, whether or not they could be considered expressions of supernatural power or rather examples of uncanny events. The basic significance of such elements in Hoffmann's writings as a whole will finally be discussed in order, it is hoped, to contribute to future reevaluations of the author's oeuvre, particularly with regards to the fantastic components of his production.

Primary Sources

The main primary source for any study of *Die Serapionsbrüder* is the short story collection itself. For this study *E.T.A. Hoffmann: Poetische Werke* (Berlin: Walter de Gruyter & Co., 1957–1960) will be used. This is the edition which has been available on a permanent basis during the time of research for this study and it will therefore be the natural source for any quotation from Hoffmann's original works. Other editions (such as for example the Aufbau-edition of Hoffmann's collected works edited by Hans Joachim Kruse) have been consulted when they have been accessible, but those more modern editions have not been used for any direct quotes of Hoffmann texts. Hartmut Steinecke's still incomplete edition of the author's collected works will of course be an invaluable resource in the future. But most of the stories discussed in this study have not yet been published in Steinecke's edition and it has therefore been impossible to use it.

Another essential primary source for any Hoffmann study are his fascinating and often insightful letters. Even the author's more personal letters often provide important information about his creative process. Sometimes he directly presents the basic idea behind a story in his letters, and his letters to his publishers are particularly interesting in that regard, since in those cases he tests his ideas on another reader.

Hoffmann's diaries are yet another source of prime importance for understanding his works. The author often uses his diaries to note creative ideas which have suddenly struck him. For this reason, they often fulfill the same function as his letters.

Some Secondary Sources

Considering the fact that E.T.A. Hoffmann is a well-known author, it goes without saying that the scholarly study of his literary production has reached enormous dimensions. It is of course impossible to discuss all aspects of this impressive body of scholarship within the framework of this study. Instead this presentation of secondary sources will focus on the more realistic goal of discussing examples of scholarship which pay particular attention to the short story collection *Die Serapionsbrüder* and the fantastic aspects of Hoffmann's production.

Lothar Pikulik's *E.T.A. Hoffmann als Erzähler*, originally intended as a commentary to accompany a planned edition of *Die Serapionsbrüder*, is an obvious point of departure when the objective is to consult secondary sources. Pikulik offers the reader background information to the Serapion tales (including the time of writing of each story, the first date and place of publication, etc.) and comprehensive data regarding the context of each narrative and a brief summary of the storyline of each account and includes comments on primary themes and useful interpretations of single works. He also offers a strongly positive assessment of the collection as a whole while emphasizing the eclectic nature of the work.

One finds a different approach in Petra Ursula Liedke-Konow's inquiry into *Die Serapionsbrüder* as presented in her *"E.T.A. Hoffmanns 'Serapionsbrüder': Eine Analyse unter zeichen- und kommunikationstheoretischen Aspekten."* This work, as the title suggests, primarily focuses on Hoffmann's short story collection from the point of view of semantic and narrative structure. As a result of this structural method, Liedke-Konow also pays a significant amount of attention to the content of the continuous frame narrative of the collection. This scholar sees the frame as a direct mirror of everything which is taking place in the individual stories.

Another Hoffmann study, Vickie Ziegler's *Bending the Frame in the German Cyclical Narrative* employs a comparative method in dealing with *Die Serapionsbrüder*. In her study, the collection is analyzed in relation to Achim von Arnim's short story anthology *Der Wintergarten*. As the title of Ziegler's study also suggests, her analysis of *Die Serapionsbrüder* sheds new light on the connection between the frame and the individual stories, a correlation which she stresses even more emphatically and consistently than Liedke-Konow does in her investigation of the same material. Ziegler maintains that the various tales in the collection should be studied in relation to the conversations in the frame rather than just being read in isolation from *Die Serapionsbrüder* as a whole.

Allienne Rimer Becker also uses a comparative approach in her examination of Hoffmann in her work *"The Fantastic in the Fiction of Hoffmann and Hawthorne."* Becker closely studies the fantastic as a genre, the background to Hoffmann's literary style as well as the narrative techniques employed in the author's fantastic production. She provides new insight into several of the writer's better known works including the novel *Die Elexire des Teufels*, the shorter *Die Doppeltgänger* and the narratives "Rat Krespel" and "Die Bergwerke zu Falun" from *Die Serapionsbrüder.*

Like Becker, William Kirk Swann approaches Hoffmann's fantastic production as a whole in his study "*The Techniques of Softening: E.T.A. Hoffmann's Presentation of the Fantastic.*" Swann examines the texts from the point of view of what he considers to be Hoffmann's technique of "softening," which he perceives as the author's way of mitigating the effects of the reader's encounters with fantastic elements in a story. Swann then divides most of Hoffmann's shorter tales into different categories according to the level of softening of the fantastic components which the author has provided in each story. It should be pointed out that Swann's approach is dependent on the reactions of the narrator or other characters within a narrative at least as much as on the response of the reader. Swann's analysis provides much stimulating and valuable material, but it should be noted that his conclusions regarding several tales (possibly due to a completely different analytical method) are radically dissimilar to the results presented in this study.

As opposed to Swann's examination of Hoffmann's œuvre as a whole, some individual stories in the author's collections have also received substantial scholarly attention. Examples such as "Rat Krespel" and "Die Bergwerke zu Falun" have already been mentioned above. Even though it is not possible to discuss all such contributions within the framework of this study, several examples deserve notice. James McGlathery's article "Der Himmel hängt ihm voller Geigen: E.T.A. Hoffmann's 'Rat Krespel', 'Die Fermate' and 'Der Baron von B.'" is significant because of its brief but lucid analysis of Hoffmann's relationship to music in a broader context. The article clarifies some of the connections between "Rat Krespel" and "Baron von B." McGlathery has more recently also published a general survey of Hoffmann's works simply called *E.T.A. Hoffmann.*

Another scholarly contribution relevant to this study is Inge Kolke's essay "Aus den Gräbern zerrst Du Deine Ätzung, teuflisches Weib!': Verwesung als strukturbildendes Element in E. T. A. Hoffmanns Vampirismus-Geschichte." Kolke's recent essay provides some new and interesting insight into a less familiar Hoffmann story.

Scholarly articles such as these exemplify an approach which emphasizes a close study of a strictly limited text material (as for instance one or several short stories) with the purpose of analyzing Hoffmann's authorship in a broader context. The theoretical method employed by some literary scholars (especially a structuralist such as Tzvetan Todorov) on the other hand tends to stress the importance of using a massive body of texts with the objective of gaining increased understanding of an entire literary oeuvre. This theoretical debate is of key significance for this study.

Chapter One
Some Theories of the Fantastic

The Evolution of Critical Thought surrounding the Fantastic

Numerous literary critics through the ages have attempted to generate a theory of fantastic fiction. Already in 1828, an anonymous French translator of Hoffmann's works made such an attempt by strongly underscoring the connection between the fantastic and the element of hesitation and doubt in the reader's mind when being confronted by a fantastic tale with a component of vagueness. The translator also suggests that such literature is not compatible with French taste which is partial to a "down to earth" style rather than clever games on the part of the author:

> Ce genre fantastique, moitié plaisant, moitié sérieux, ce jeu d'imagination que ne semble avoir autre but que l'activité même de cette faculté, ce vague qui laisse le lecteur en doute s'il se trouve dans le monde reél or dans les régions de merveilleux, tout cela est peu goûté en France où l'on veut du positif et où le lecteur se sent peut disposé à servir en quelque sorte de jouet à l'auteur.[1]

This emphasis on the reader's hesitation regarding the setting of a text in the real world or in a supernatural milieu has often been used to identify the fantastic as a genre based on ambiguity, an element which makes it impossible to ascertain in which realm (our authentic existence or an imagined world) events actually occur. The concept of the marvelous ("le merveilleux") is of key importance in establishing a definition of the fantastic and has often returned in the scholarly debate. French literary critics in particular have been preoccupied with developing a theory of the fantastic along these lines.

French fascination with Hoffmann's production was seriously initiated when, as, among others, a scholar like Allienne Rimer Becker has also noted, Dr. Johann Ferdinand Koreff, one of the author's close friends, relocated to Paris a short time after the writer had passed away in the summer of 1822.[2]

Being an often seen guest in the most prestigious French literary salons, Koreff familiarized the Parisian authors and critics with the tales of Hoffmann. Captivated by Koreff's descriptions of Hoffmann and his literary production, Adolphe-François Loeve-Veimars, a journalist of German origin, began translating the writer's works. The first of his volumes, book one of *Contes fantastiques*, was published in 1829. Hoffmann became a famous author in France and the critics lauded his fiction, while portraying him as the gifted creator of a novel kind of literature. Hoffmann's success in France, in the view of the literary historian

Marcel Breuillac, could be explained by his founding of a new "intermediary" genre with a new approach to reality and fantasy. Breuillac refers to it as "un genre intermédiaie entre le merveilleux proprement dit et le réel." French and other scholars have often discussed whether Hoffmann really was the creator of the genre of the fantastic, and what the genre encompasses. Some, such as Breuillac, maintain that he is the originator, while others are somewhat more hesitant in their judgments. A critic such as Jean Ricci belongs to the latter group. In an article published in *Études Germaniques* in 1951, Ricci still seems inclined to credit Hoffmann with the genre while at the same time urging caution. He states:

> Ce fantastique à base de doute, existe-t-il depuis longtemps? ou est-ce une invention récente? Il est difficile d'affirmer ce qui demanderait une enquête à travers les siècles. Pourtant, on serait tenté de croire que c'est Hoffmann qui, par une intuition géniale, l'aurait invité: l'incrédulité propagée par le rationalisme du XVIIIe siècle aurait rendu nécessaire ce nouveau mode de merveilleux.

Apart from pointing out this relationship between the fantastic and the criticism of the weaknesses of rationalism, Ricci especially underscores the connection between the fantastic and the Romantic period while emphasizing the fact that the genre tended to get out of fashion with the decline of Romanticism: "Le genre tombe en désuétude après le romantisme: il n'inspire plus personne, le public s'en détourne, tous ces mondes merveilleux, l'Atlantide, Urdargarten, Djinnistan, Famagusta se sont démodés." ("Le Fantastique...," 116). Commenting on the extraordinary success of Hoffmann's "Der goldne Topf," Ricci addresses the question of the function of the fantastic, an issue which literary critics still debate: should the fantastic teach a moral, sociological or aesthetic lesson? This critic formulates the question as follows: "En somme, le fantastique servirait à dissimuler le substantifique moelle de Rabelais?" ("Le Fantastique..." 116).

Several other critics have attempted to answer this same question, some suggesting that the fantastic serves to contain a more profound meaning, others proposing that its only purpose is to entertain the reader.

In his study *Le conte fantastique en France de Nodier à Maupassant*, Pierre-Georges Castex, who approaches the fantastic from a psychological perspective, sharply differs with Breuillac and Ricci regarding Hoffmann's role as the creator of the fantastic genre. Castex instead maintains that the minor French author Jacques Cazotte is the real originator of the genre. Cazotte wrote the narrative *Le diable amoureux*, a work in which the author suggests rational explanations for curious incidents that occur in the story, while at the time reserving the possibility of supernatural explanations. Cazotte therefore, according to Castex, invented the genre.[3] But a connection between Cazotte and Hoffmann is also proposed:

Il nous paraît important de noter cette filiation; ainsi le maître incontesté du conte fantastique européen a puisé lui-même, pour quelques-unes de ses pages les plus étranges, dans l'œuvres modestes et féconde d'un précurseur français. (Castex 41)

Cazotte's impact on Hoffmann's fiction has been recognized by most critics since 1980, when Johann Cerny pointed out Hoffmann's debt to the French writer, whom he read and even mentioned in his works. But even though he may have borrowed from Cazotte, the German author is nonetheless generally considered the father of the French school of the fantastic. Commenting on Hoffmann's influence on French literature, Marcel Schneider, asserts that this author showed the way: "Hoffmann a ouvert la voie, il a indiqué le chemin: après lui chacun se précipite."[4]

The road which Hoffmann thus opened for literature is firmly based on the use of everyday reality as the setting for bizarre occurrences as represented in his fiction and those who imitate his works. This fact is also stressed by Castex who makes a clear distinction between the genre of the fantastic and the genre of traditional mythology which is founded on a completely artificially created world of imagination: "Le fantastique, en effet, ne se confond pas avec l'affabulation conventionelle des récits mythologiques ou des fééries qui implique un depaysement de l'esprit." (Castex 8) Castex continues his analysis by emphasizing the idea of the fantastic as a brutal intrusion into everyday life. This intrusion, he concludes, is based on morbid states of consciousness where mental processes such as nightmares and delirium play a significant part:

Il se caractérise au contraire par une intrusion brutale du mystère dans le cadre de la vie réelle; il est lié généralement aux états morbides de la conscience qui, dans les phénomènes de cauchemar ou délire, projette devant elle de images de ses angoisses ou de ses terreurs. (Castex 8)

The conclusion of this definition appears to be that one learns more about the author's state of mind than about the literary text. Castex also often comes back to the idea that the fantastic is more conspicuous in modern literature than in other earlier periods due to the especially neurotic nature of the world today. It is interesting to contrast this view with that of a somewhat more recent scholar, Tzvetan Todorov, who maintains that the fantastic has disappeared from modern fiction.[5]

The assumption made by Castex that the fantastic is characterized by a brutal encroachment on everyday reality of a mystery which can be explained either rationally or supernaturally, closely parallels the opinion of Roger Caillois, who expresses basically the same idea in his *Anthologie*. In his view, the fantastic is something which becomes an almost insufferable interruption of normal everyday life:

Le féerique est un univers merveilleux qui s'oppose au monde réel sans en détruire la cohérence. Le fantastique, au contraire, manifeste un scandale, une déchirure, une irruption insolite, presque insupportable dans le monde réel.[6]

Even though both Castex and Caillois maintain that the genre of the fantastic is distinguished by the intrusion of something peculiar into the world of reality, Caillois, who considers the fantastic a game with the sentiment of fear, ("un jeu avec la peur"), bases his theory, as it is presented in the study *Images, Images*, on the relationship which is built in the text between the reader and the author.[7] Realistic works convey a distinct message for author and reader. Marvelous works have a message which is apparent to the author, but remains ambiguous to the reader. Fantastic works, on the other hand, are those in which the message is obscure for both reader and author. (*Anthologie* 9–16) Caillois regards (as do for instance Ricci and Castex) the fantastic as a compensation for the perceived excessive rationalism of the Enlightenment period. He also agrees with those of his colleagues who consider Hoffmann the first indisputable master of the genre. The masterpieces of this type of literature, he notes, were written from the time of Hoffmann up until about 1850, when this type of fiction declined in public appeal. (*Anthologie* 16) It should be noted that Caillois reaches his definition of the fantastic by analyzing the fairy tale and defining which components exist in this genre but not in fantastic fiction. This definition seems to work backwards. It presupposes that one already knows what fantastic fiction is and only has to look for the ingredients that make it what it is already known to be.

Another scholar, Louis Vax, essentially shares the views presented by Castex and Caillois, but he also believes that the definition of the fantastic has not yet been fully formulated. In his essay "L'Art de faire peur," Vax echoes his colleagues in defining the fantastic as an intrusion on everyday reality: "—irruption d'un élément terrifiant dans un monde rassurant et soumis à la raison." By interpreting the genre of the fantastic in such a way, Vax, in part, bases his categorization of fantastic fiction on the sentiments and reactions of the reader, who ultimately must be the one who determines whether or not a terrifying component has actually appeared in the text.

Having supplied a brief basic definition of the nature of the fantastic, Vax approaches the genre as an aesthetic expression of man's primitive superstitions. He concludes that when man no longer takes his superstitions seriously, he manipulates them to create art. ("l'Art...," 934) While playing on man's primitive superstitious anxieties, a good fantastic narrative is terrifying, but it is also aesthetically pleasing as an art form. Being aimed at the incredulous reader, it endeavors not to be believable but entertaining and is intended to provide "psychic nutrition" by kindling a "peculiar sentiment" in those who no longer believe in the supernatural. ("l'Art ...," 917)

Another aspect of the fantastic, according to Vax, is the fact that the fantastic story is arranged around a motif; the critic examines it by studying its content, searching for such elements as vampires or phantoms. Vax strongly underscores the importance of such motifs:

> On admet couramment que c'est à son motif qu'un conte doit son caractère fantastique. Certains motifs seraient fantastiques, d'autres non. Un conte fantastique, c'est une histoire de vampire, de revenant, de loup-garou ..., et non une histoire de fleur ou d'oisseau. Un classement des motifs donnera une esquisse du monde fantastique.[8]

Vax contends that one should not attempt to explain a work allegorically or try to psychoanalyze it in order to give it a lucid meaning. Such an approach would destroy the intended ambiguity, a fundamental part of the enjoyment of the tale. In other words, if one deciphers the fantastic, one annihilates it. Fantastic works and themes should thus not, according to this critic, be analyzed by Freudian psychology, although they may often have sexual connotations. (*Séduction* 308)

The fantastic could also be considered a rebellion against the notion of reality. The imagination is given free rein even though the fantastic takes place in a seemingly realistic environment. The most successful fantastic writer is like the most successful liar since he is the one who magnifies reality the least. ("l'Art ...," 1030) The typical ambiguity of the genre even extends to the fundamental moral attitude of a story, since ambiguity, Vax insists, is inclined to generate ambivalence towards moral issues. (l'Art..., 1026–27) The components of the fantastic suggested by Vax seem greatly subjective in nature. They appear to be dependent, at least to a great extent, on the "sang-froid" of the reader. It is easy to find works that include supernatural intrusions into everyday reality but which do not cause fear. Such writings do not belong to any genre acknowledged by Vax, and, in spite of being closely related to his concept of the fantastic, apparently serve no specific literary function.

In part as a result of such weaknesses, the theories presented by Louis Vax have met opposition. Claude Roy, for instance, maintains that the fantastic is not primarily a revolt against reality. Instead, he claims, the genre is a revolt against death. Roy's definition of the fantastic as "inquiétude sourde" implies an identification with man's sense of sin and forbidden fruit. A fear of condemnation and judgment thereby becomes a key element in understanding the fantastic:

> Mais le fantastique, c'est-à-dire l'inquiétude sourde, l'angoisse ou la terreur, surgissant avec le sentiment du ce n'est pas bien, avec la notion de

condamnation ou d'autocondamnation, de reproche ou d'autoreproche. Le
fantastique est étroitement lié à la notion de mal, de péché, d'interdit.[9]

Fantastic fiction portrays man as possessing an instinct for death and destruction;
but it is, Roy asserts, counterbalanced by an opposing instinct for life and
creativity. Since the genre of the fantastic depicts man's rebellion against his finite
condition, which knowledge and science expose, it is natural to have a
comprehensive production of fantastic fiction during a period which included an
incredible development of technology and experimental sciences, such as was the
case in the nineteenth century. (Roy 1401) Such a theory would also explain the
popularity of the fantastic at the present time.

Much of the discussion surrounding a definition of the fantastic has essentially
followed the pattern outlined above in recent decades. One scholar who has
attempted to contribute to the theoretical debate while choosing a slightly different
angle is Tzvetan Todorov whose structuralist models deserve special attention.

The Contribution of Tzvetan Todorov

The Bulgarian-French structuralist theoretician Tzvetan Todorov has offered
a detailed definition of the fantastic. As a structuralist, he emphasizes the basic
structure of a literary work rather than the details of the content. Todorov's work
in the area of the fantastic is comprehensive and has been the subject of an
extensive debate. His main contribution to the discussion is the study *Introduction
à la littérature fantastique* (first published in 1970). His definition of this literary
phenomenon has many advantages. First of all, it is fairly precise. It allows a
relatively clear determination of which literary production falls within the concept
of the fantastic and which falls outside. Moreover, it presents a reasonably coherent
representation of literary genres in general, providing a comparison of the fantastic
with similar genres. Todorov's definition does not rely on the personal emotional
response of a particular reader to discover the fantastic elements, but instead
depends on intra-textual indicators to understand the nature of the work. It is also
important to underscore the fact that Todorov's definition deals with a particular
attitude towards reality and literature.

Todorov offers three essential conditions for fantastic literature. He initially
postulates the existence of a fantastic occurrence. In a world like our own, the one
with which we are familiar, a world without supernatural beings such as devils and
vampires, an inexplicable event occurs: "Dans un monde qui est bien le nôtre, celui
que nous connaissons, sans diables, sylphides, ni vampires, se produit une
événement qui ne peut s'expliquer par les lois de ce même monde familier."
(Todorov 29) It is not this occurrence that defines the literary genre, however. Of
fundamental importance is the literary perception of the happening. The fantastic
holds the duration of the uncertainty between two different resolutions to such an

event. Todorov concludes: "Le concept de fantastique se définit donc par rapport à ceux de réel et d'imaginaire." (Todorov 29)

The fantastic suggests an integration of the reader into the world of the fictional personalities, and that world is defined by the reader's indefinite perception of the related occurrences. An occurrence regarded as inconceivable according to the laws of empirical reality actually takes place and the text fails to give a lucid answer as to whether the incident is to be considered natural or supernatural. The reader's hesitation is thus the first condition of the fantastic. It is the condition of ambiguity which primarily separates Todorov's definition of the fantastic from those of most other critics.

This scholar also presents two other conditions. He emphasizes that most fantastic fiction involves identification with a specific character who hesitates in interpreting an occurrence. It is this character who falters in defining the real nature of the fantastic phenomenon. This specific condition is not, however, an absolute criterion of the genre, but rather represents the manner in which the ambiguity is normally demonstrated by the author. (Todorov 36)

Todorov's third condition of the fantastic (in this case fully concurring with the definition presented by Vax) is that the reading of fantastic material can be neither poetic nor allegorical. (Todorov 36–37) The fantastic presupposes a literal reading and must supply intra-textual indications that it is to be taken literally. In isolation it is not clear how to interpret a sentence such as "The water ran silver to the beach." A poetic reading of the sentence simply implies the visual impact on the viewer or reader; the literal reading suggests that silver rather than water flowed into the sea or lake which is depicted. The latter reading alone can involve the concept of the fantastic. The final condition, in other words, presupposes that the inconceivable or supernatural occurrence can be "real" within the boundaries of the story line. Todorov further maintains that not all fiction and not all literal meanings are linked to the fantastic, but the fantastic is nonetheless linked to both concepts. He concludes: "Toute fiction, tout sens littéral ne sont pas liés au fantastique; mais tout fantastique est lié à la fiction et au sens littéral. Ceux-ci sont donc des conditions pour l'existence du fantastique." (Todorov 80)

In order for a genre to have significance, it must be separable from other similar literary genres. Todorov regards the fantastic as a part of a series of literary genres which include manifest breaches of the natural or rational order. He mentions two genres lying on either side of the fantastic which he calls the "uncanny" ("l'étrange pur") and the "marvelous" ("le merveilleux pur"). The uncanny involves literary works in which circumstances are described which may be easily explained by the laws of reason, but which are, nevertheless, in some way, implausible, remarkable, astonishing, exceptional or unexpected. (Todorov 51–52) Todorov admits that such a definition is ambiguous, and proceeds to propose that this is not really a genre but rather a category confined on one extreme by the fantastic and dissolving in its other extreme into the common domain of literature. (Todorov 52) When discussing these definitions it should be noted that it is not clear what Todorov means by the latter concept and that makes this particular part of his theoretical system troublesome and incomplete. A comprehensive and detailed treatment of this problem is beyond the scope of this study, but the issue will be addressed further when recent criticism of Todorov's ideas is discussed.

The uncanny, as explained above, functions as a demarcation to the fantastic. At the other end of the continuum there exists a genre which Todorov refers to as the marvelous. The marvelous is a genre in which supernatural components evoke no special response either in the fictional characters or in the implicit reader of the narrative. It is not an attitude toward the occurrences depicted which denotes the marvelous, but rather the nature of these happenings. (Todorov 59) The view of the supernatural powers is primarily dependent on the reader's individual outlook on reality. Todorov exemplifies this important distinction with the existence of exotic animals in *The Arabian Nights*. The beasts described there might not necessarily have been marvelous to the intended audience, and only the modern readership would consider these passages marvelous. (Todorov 60) In the genre of the marvelous, the empirically unimaginable is accepted without amazement as part of the normal order.

The borders between the fantastic and its adjoining genres are not exact. Intermediate categories referred to as the "fantastic-uncanny" ("le fantastique-étrange") and the "fantastic-marvelous" ("le fantastique-merveilleux") also constitute elements of Todorov's theoretical framework. In these sub-genres, this hesitation or fantastic ambiguity is upheld for a period of the reading, but the uncertainty is ultimately resolved in favor of either a natural or unnatural explanation of the event, thus moving the narrative into either the uncanny or the marvelous. (Todorov 49)

One significant result of the change in perspective is that the genre of the fantastic is delimited according to a temporary linear course through a given text. On an initial reading, a text may be fantastic until the conclusion, when an entirely natural explanation may be offered for a certain incident. An this point, the narrative changes into the uncanny. Any subsequent reading of the story will include no ambiguity or vagueness and will render the text completely uncanny. The genre into which a literary work falls is therefore, according to Todorov, both reader-specific and time-specific. (Todorov 93–94)

Todorov concludes his discussion of the two "boundary genres" by explaining that the real goal of the marvelous is the complete examination of universal reality. To express this idea, he borrows the following quote from Pierre Mabel's *Le miroir du merveilleux*: "le but réel du voyage merveilleux est, nous sommes déjà en mesure de comprendre, l'exploration plus totale de la réalité universelle." (Todorov 62) Todorov offers no theory, however, as to what the real goal of the uncanny or fiction in general might be. These are, in brief, the main features of Todorov's definition of the fantastic. His study also contains analyses of the narrative technique through which fantastic ambiguity is created and of the importance of the fantastic as a facet of the total literary production.

Todorov's theory of the genre of the fantastic has been frequently debated and possibly more criticized than actually employed. It has been said that his system is not complete. It does not cover all texts and does not explain all expressions of the fantastic in fiction. It also, it is said, falters in addressing important questions about literature in general. The most common criticism of Todorov's definition clearly refers to this perceived incompleteness of his study. It has furthermore been suggested that he has used a very limited selection of sample texts and has therefore not satisfactorily attempted to apply his definition to non-French, non-modern texts. It has also been pointed out that Todorov fails to distinguish the role of the fantastic in the short story from that in the novel. It has been proposed that he would have reached a different definition of the fantastic if he had used other texts for his analysis of the genre.[10]

It is true that Todorov confines his study to a selection of approximately thirty literary works. These works are chosen essentially from the French, English and Russian traditions. One should note, however, that Todorov's definition of the fantastic is entirely theoretical. It would define a genre even if not a single literary contribution could be found which exemplified this particular genre. The proper test of this analytical model would be to search for and to analyze those texts that meet Todorov's criteria, rather than to simply conclude that many works fail to meet these requirements.

In addition to analyzing the nature of Todorov's highly abstract structural theory, it is essential to underscore that he sees the fantastic as an expression of the bad conscience of the nineteenth century considering its interest in such subjects as incest, sadism, rape, necrophilia, vampires, death and other themes that were forbidden in the literature of realism. By attributing sexual immoderation and deviations to the impact of the devil, the fantastic author was able to approach topics that were otherwise taboo. Todorov maintains that modern psychoanalysis has replaced fantastic fiction because it examines sexual subjects and discusses them openly. (Todorov 167) The conclusion drawn from such an assertion must be that the genre of the fantastic no longer exists since psychoanalysis has eradicated the need for it, a notion which must appear totally invalid for most modern readers and critics, who would probably consider the fantastic very much a still active genre.

In part referring to subjects dealt with by modern psychoanalysis, Todorov addresses some significant themes in fantastic literature. He approaches them by focusing on what he regards as two main aspects of the fantastic, one is labeled the "self" ("je") and the other is referred to as the "other" ("tu"). Themes of the "self" could be considered defined by the relation between man and the surrounding the world, of the perception-conscience system (a Freudian term): "Nous avons vu qu'on pouvait interpréter les thèmes de *je* comme autant de mises en ouvre de la relation entre l'homme et le monde, du système perception-conscience." (Todorov 146) Perception (and especially vision) is a key to the understanding of such themes. In the fantastic, the problematic nature of perceiving reality is emphasized. This includes self-perception. The "Doppelgänger"-motif (quite important in E.T.A. Hoffmann's works) would, for instance, fit into this category. The multiplication of personality is a result of the transition between matter and spirit and we become several persons even physically: "La multiplication de la personalité, prise en lettre, est une conséquence immédiate du passage possible entre matière et esprit: on est plusieurs personnes mentalement, on le devient physiquement." (Todorov 122)

Themes of the "other" concern the relation of man with his desire, and thereby with his subconscious. Desire and its variations, cruelty, pain and fear included, commonly represents the relations between human beings. In the genre of the fantastic, such elements are illustrated by supernatural images which constitute physical manifestations of the "other." Supernatural beings such as vampires and werewolves thus fit naturally into this category. (Todorov 146)

Todorov's division into two main groups appears somewhat questionable, and the suggested nomenclature seems reversed. The themes of "self" appear to include the relationship with the larger community of the real world, themes of the "other" seem to involve the extension of the "self." Todorov's choice of terms and their definition also apparently relies on the popular assumption that human emotional responses are completely conditional upon outside incitements.

Human fear of snakes, for example, would be a case in point. Todorov would regard such anxiety as a theme of the other. There is something inborn in a snake that provokes fright and abhorrence in a person who is afraid of such creatures. Snakes are, in other words, so odious that it makes the fear of them independent of any qualities in the person dreading them, and uncanny works in which snakes incites repulsion in human beings would include themes of the other. If, on the other hand, the snakes are considered emotionally uninvolved objects and it is presumed instead that the anxiety they arouse is conditional upon the subject reacting to them, the same uncanny works would be classified as involving themes of the self.

Another example can further illustrate this point. Todorov approaches the sexual drive as an element emerging from the other. Sexual desire is thus not a mental construct of men. It is rather something inherent in women, who are considered desirable objects. Addressing sexuality and other sensual phenomena in terms of being components outside the subject makes Todorov's division of themes highly problematic.

Even though Todorov cites various themes of fantastic fiction, it should be noted that he does not necessarily offer any comprehensive analysis of them. The reason for this lack of detailed inquiry into the nature of the themes is the fact that his approach to the genre is that of the structuralist formalist for whom it is enough to indicate the existence of a configuration of the themes as a part of the structural arrangement of the fantastic as a genre.

One of the authorships that, at least to a great extent, would fit into this structuralist theoretical system is that of E.T.A. Hoffmann. The literary production of this author contains many of the elements which Todorov touches upon. But the sometimes sharp criticism aimed at Todorov's contributions to literary theory needs to be addressed also with the objective of a better understanding of Hoffmann's role in the creation of fantastic literature. A substantial part of the recent debate on the nature of fantastic literature has been devoted to a critical discussion of Todorov's structuralist approach to the genre and several alternative theories have been provided by several scholars and writers of fiction.

Some Aspects of the Debate on Fantastic Literature

Todorov's contributions have been evaluated both in a positive and a negative way. Essentially positive to Todorov's theory is another scholar belonging to the same structuralist tradition, Jean Bellemin-Noël, who has basically the same fundamental definition of the fantastic in mind as does his colleague. Bellemin-Noël maintains that the genre of the fantastic is a specific way of telling a story: "Le fantastique est une manière de raconter, le fantastique est structuré comme le fantasme." He alsotypifies a structuralist approach by underscoring that an analysis of the fantastic should be founded on the form of a text rather than its content: "Il importe de souligner notre définition du fantastique 'structuré' comme le fantasme. C'est une forme que l'on recherche, non un contenu." (Bellemin-Noël 7)

A fantastic tale, structured as a psychological fantasy, is fashioned by the utilization of precise techniques which Bellemin-Noël calls "fantasmagoriques." (Bellemin-Noël 3) Among the fantastic effects that identify the genre are: (1) the "mis en abîme," in which the fantastic story speaks of its own writing and of writing in general; (2) "l'effet de miroir," in which a second narrative, in reduced proportions, is embedded in the tale and mirrors the main plot; (3) "l'effet du fantastique proprement dit," which employs in the narrative the word "fantastique" or phrases such as "regards phosphoriques" or "rires sardoniques"; (4)"l'effet de citation" by which the text refers to other writers of fantastic works, with Hoffmann being the master who is consistently cited; (5) "autoréférence implicite," by which an author refers to his other fantastic production in order to create a fantastic world for his readers.

This continuation and development of the structuralist theories as represented by Todorov and others are not accepted by a critic like Roxanne Eminescu, who also criticizes the older French theoretical tradition which equally emphasizes the hesitation of the reader regarding the nature of the supernatural as a fundamental element in the genre. Eminescu instead contends that the determining factor of the fantastic is the malaise which the reader feels even after the mystery has been solved. As a result of his or her confrontation with the supernatural, the reader to some degree loses confidence in the known natural world. Eminescu positions the fantastic in an area between literature which is structured according to laws of reality and that which is not, so that the fantastic account might refer either to the real world or to a supernatural world. She states this notion in the following way:

> L'ambiguïté du fantastique provient de sa double nature, rattaché simultanément à deux mondes disjoints. Le lecteur du récit fantastique essaye en vain de reconnaître le monde dans lequel il est introduit; il s'y sent mal à liaise en ne le reconnaissant point et, après avoir conçu du soupçon à tour contre le personnage et contre l'auteur il accède à ce degré supérieur de la méfiance ou, perdant confiance dans le monde connu, il accepte l'existence de l'autre monde qui'il redoûtait.[11]

By classifying the ways in which a connection is made in the text between the two worlds which exist simultaneously within it, Eminescu supplies a schema for analyzing fantastic works. She moreover concludes that Todorov is mistaken in excluding poetry from the fantastic. (Eminescu 211)

Even though Jacques Finné, agreeing with Eminescu, does not want to exclude poetry from the genre of the fantastic, he does not discuss it in his study *La littérature fantastique*, but limits his analysis to the novel and the novella. Finné proposes that the fantastic illustrates an impossibility which happens in the midst of everyday life, but he excludes from his "fantastique canonique" any literature which is not written simply to entertain: "Le fantastique est donc une forme de l'art pour l'art, un jeu, une gratuité, non un tremplin."[12] The fantastic can, according to such a definition, never be didactic. As a result of this, the works of Cazotte are eliminated from Finné's canon of fantastic writings, since they are regarded as "lessons in theology." Examples of the so-called "neo-fantastique" are also excluded. With this term Finné refers to any literature which is intended to spread ideas such as psychological or philosophical relativism. (Finné 15) In Finné's system, fantastic writings are classified according to the manner in which the author has structured the explanation given for mysterious occurrences in the narrative—either by (1) a rational explanation; (2) a supernatural explanation; or (3) an ambiguous explanation. Moreover, the fantastic work has a structure like the classical periodic sentence, with its protasis and apodosis. (Finné 173)

The protasis includes (1) a realistic introduction, (2) mysteries, and (3) a supernatural explanation, while the apodosis is the narrative exploitation of the components of the protasis. By employing this system of organization, Finné is able to distinguish the fantastic from the genres of the detective story, science-fiction, and tales in which the supernatural is rationally explained.

French literary theory, which has traditionally regarded the fantastic as a separate genre, has aspired to analyze its content and structure. Most modern French critics have rejected allegorical and philosophical interpretations of fantastic works. The fundamental features of Todorov's structuralist approach have gained the upper hand in recent French literary criticism dealing with the fantastic even though certain parts of his system have been severely criticized. Contemporary scholars have, like Todorov, explored the structure of the fantastic narrative, each having devised his or her method. Even though French genre theory has formed the basis of much modern research on the fantastic, no French scholars have, to date, produced a complete theory of the fantastic, one which would encompass its full range.

As part of a major renunciation of the modern French critical tradition, the Polish science fiction author Stanislaw Lem mounts a vigorous assault on Todorov's definition of the fantastic. After explaining, in an introduction to his article "Todorov's fantastic theory of literature," that his objective is to discredit structuralism in literary scholarship by dissecting Todorov's study, Lem depicts French structuralism as "a retrograde trend" in French critical thought, which aiming at nothing less than logical infallibility in theory-building, transformed itself into an incorrigible dogmatism.[13]

While strongly castigating Todorov for choosing representative examples upon which to build his theory, Lem declares that in literature representative samples are not the same as they are in the natural sciences. Todorov, Lem contends, is proceeding on a false premise in deriding the literary critic who would "engage in endless reading of actual works before beginning to define a genre. Every normal tiger is representative for that species of cats, but there is no such thing as a 'normal story.'" (Lem 228)

Lem also notes that there are only two science-fiction tales in Todorov's selection. There is nothing from modern fantasy. Moreover, there is no room for subgenera of the fantastic. Nor is there any room for "fantastic philosophy" or "fantastic history." Lem accuses Todorov of selecting "representative samples" of the fantastic to fit his Procrustean bed and of failing to account for all fantastic literature, since "a theory of literature either embraces all works or it is not a theory." Lem continues: "A theory of works weeded out in advance by means beyond its compass constitutes not generalization but its contrary, that is particularization." (Lem 236) He then explains this statement:

One cannot when theorizing discriminate *beforehand* against a certain group of works, i.e. not bring them under the scope of analysis at all. A taxonomically oriented theory can set up a hierarchy in its subject matter, i.e. assign non uniform values to the elements of the entire set under investigation, but it should do this openly, on the sly, and throughout its whole domain, showing what sort of criteria it employs for making distinctions and how they perform their tasks of evaluation. (Lem 236–37)

Lem also argues that Todorov fails to take into account the aesthetic component of literature. His system fails to differentiate between "good" and "bad" literature and therefore provides no effective tool for the critic. (Lem 237) As long as the fantastic is analyzed in terms of its impact on the reader, it makes no sense to exclude the artistic success of a writer from the examination of a work. The study of literature then becomes a quasi-scientific analysis of a rather limited number of attributes of a text rather than any meaningful understanding of an artistic whole.

Even though Lem regards Todorov's theories as arbitrary and deficient, he does not undertake the challenging task of attempting to formulate his own theory of the fantastic. Other Polish scholars and critics, however, have made significant theoretical contributions. An approach which is fundamentally different from that of the French school of thought is taken by W. Ostrowski, who considers the fantastic as a departure from the traditional conventions of Realism rather than a separate genre. In realistic writings, the world of fiction is based on familiar reality, but not so in the fantastic. Ostrowski explains:

> Fantastic fiction is produced by a transformation of constituents of the empirical world and/or their patterns, which makes them so different from common experience that we may look for them in this world in vain, or that their existence is, at least, objectively verifiable. They exist in their literary form as products of the imagination or fantasy and for this reason are called fantastic.[14]

A substantial contribution of Polish scholarship are the critical studies of Andrzej Zgorzelski, who defines the fantastic as "a breach of intra textual laws," since in a fantastic text the author breaks the laws of the fictional world which he has established in his story. By breaking his own narrative laws, the author creates a new genre "which is marked by the existence of two models of reality in the text." (Zgorzelski 299) This definition clearly contrasts with that of Caillois and some other scholars, who maintain that the fantastic constitutes a breaking of the rules of the *real* world, with a resulting shock or surprise on the part of the reader.

To fully grasp Zgorzelski's theory, one must first understand that, to this scholar, genre is a diachronic system which manifests itself in a sequence of syntactic structures that diverge from each other very little when only contiguous ones are studied. Genres thus undergo an evolutionary process and develop into new genres and subgenres. Science fiction, for instance, can be said to have evolved from the fantastic. (Zgorzelski 299)

During the evolution of a genre, the popular motifs connected with it change. The motifs in the fantastic narrative, such as ghosts, vampires or mad scientists, "aim at provoking the reader's feeling of wonder, of the unexpected and the unknown." (Zgorzelski 299)   The evolution of the genre also entails a loss of a shock value where it originally existed. The shock value instead becomes part of the internal structure of a new genre. The case of vampire stories could be used as an example to illustrate this idea. The original tales of Count Dracula had a distinct surprise value of their own, leaving one of the protagonists in the novel *Dracula* shocked at the appearance of a vampire in modern times, but generations of works belonging to this popular tradition create an expectation that a traveler in Transylvania at some point will face vampires.

The evolution of a genre can also be dependent on a didactic process. By *not* excluding the didactic from the fantastic, Zgorzelski puts himself in a different camp from that of the French structuralists who insist that the fantastic must not be a vehicle for didactic messages. The opposition to Todorov's definition for instance, becomes evident in Zgorzelski's analysis.

Zgorzelski's definition of the genre has some undeniable advantages. It provides for a fairly exact determination of which works belong to the fantastic and combines a theoretical framework with a literary-historical framework. It seems to avoid subjective concerns and difficulties of narrative perspective which tend to demolish other definitions. But questions still remain. The precise manner in which rules are established is somewhat vague. Are such rules dependent on the reader's perception of reality? It is furthermore not entirely clear what function this genre serves, which makes the distinction between the fantastic and other genres seem trivial.

Zgorzelski is not alone in thinking along these lines. Conceding that his definition of the fantastic is somewhat identical to that of the American scholar Eric S. Rabkin, he points out that his concept of genre is quite different, suggesting that his American colleague uses a broader concept. (Zgorzelski 300) The theory of the fantastic proposed in Rabkin's study *The Fantastic in Literature* does indeed have many similarities with Zgorzelski's ideas. But Rabkin uses a different terminology in his analytical approach to the genre. He gives a succinct definition of the fantastic: "The fantastic is a quality of astonishment that we feel when the ground rules of a narrative world are suddenly made to turn about 180 degrees."[15] He continues: "We recognize this reversal in the reactions of the characters, the statements of narrators, and the implications of the structure, all playing on and against our whole experience as readers." (Rabkin 41)

The fantastic, the "anti-expected," Rabkin concludes, has a place in any genre, but the genre to which the fantastic is central is the class of literature or film or any other medium which makes the consideration of fantastic reversals its very heart. (Rabkin 217) Rabkin positions literature on a continuum, with reality at one end and fantasy on the other. Detective stories, science fiction, and satirical works, for instance, are placed on his continuum because they all make unexpected reversals in their narrative ground rules. By using such a continuum one is able to compare the degree of the fantastic in a detective story with that in a science fiction tale or a utopian account. Science fiction, satire and utopian fiction constitute a "supergenre." Rabkin maintains that such an approach offers helpful and interesting insights into genre theory. His bent toward structuralism manifests itself in his utilization of terms such as "langue," "parole" and "graholecet."

An advantage with the fantastic genre, according to Rabkin, is that it can offer escape from boredom since it is able to provide "a message of psychological consolation." (Rabkin 73) Moreover, it is a fundamental mode of human knowledge and not only a literary phenomenon for people who are trapped in the prisons of their own minds. Man's "glory," Rabkin concludes, is that he is not bound by reality but "travels in fantastic worlds" (Rabkin 225)

Rabkin's study is only one of several significant American contributions to the debate. American scholarship has explored the fantastic from many different viewpoints. Contributions have been made by representatives of various schools of literary criticism, such as the structuralist, mythopoetic, Marxist, and classical. A substantive theory of the fantastic based on a mythopoetic approach has been presented by Gary K. Wolfe in his essay "Symbolic Fantasy" published in 1975. Wolfe explores the fantastic and connects much of it with Northrop Frye's concept of the romance.[16] Nonetheless, he considers fantasy a separate genre, with his fundamental concept of a genre taken from Wellek and Warren's *Theory of Literature*.

Since much of fantastic fiction includes components of myths, Wolfe confines his study to mythopoetic fantasy, a subgenre of fantasy which he labels "symbolic fantasy." This subgenre has the following traits: (1) The protagonist is often possessed of a certain naivete towards life; he is often visionary, artistic, quiet and scholarly. He may approach heroic stature, but he might also be apt to be cynical and embittered and close to middle age. (2) The hero is stripped of a vice or an illusion by a process of education. (3) The narrative takes place in a world that is spiritually analogue to our own. (4) In the end, the hero is transformed and returns to his own world. (Wolfe 205) Such a literature is useful for presenting moral and spiritual values in a way which realistic works cannot. It is interesting to note that Wolfe here joins forces with those who emphasize the didactic function of the fantastic. Wolfe also stresses that fantasy, at least of the mythopoetic kind, arises when the dominant cultural attitude of a generation grows so narrow that it fails to account for, or to provide sufficient means for, the expression of any significant aspect of man's psychological or spiritual makeup. (Wolfe 205) He concludes: "Thus the study of mythopoetic fantasy must be the study of individual created myths, involving the acceptance of the value-experience and in many cases the entire artificial cosmology of the myth's creator." (Wolfe 208)

Even though Wolfe's thoughts do not constitute a comprehensive theory of the fantastic, they underscore components which had previously been overlooked. The mythopoetic elements in Hoffmann's writings, for instance, have been the subject of substantial literary criticism.

The theory of another American scholar, W.R. Irwin, as he presents it in his study *The Game of the Impossible*, is similar to that of the Polish scholar Ostrowski. Irwin, like Ostrowski, rejects the notion of the fantastic as a separate genre. He instead asserts that the fantastic can be present in any kind of imaginative literature. Fantastic works, he maintains, simply contain certain thematic elements. (Irwin 8–9) In Irwin's view, the fantastic is a "game," a conspiracy of intellectual subversiveness into which the reader and author knowingly enter. (Irwin 9) For him, the fantastic exists when the persuasive establishment and development of an impossibility occurs in a work of fiction. (Irwin 10) This definition would eliminate a large part of Hoffmann's production, since it typically does not persuasively establish an impossibility, but leaves the reader in a state of hesitation as to whether or not an "impossibility" has actually happened.

Irwin's definition resembles that of representatives of French scholarship, particularly Finné, who also contend that fantasy is a game. One should also remember Caillois' theory that the fantastic is a game with fear ("un jeu avec la peur"). As opposed to the French critics however, (but similarly to, for example, Ostrowski), Irwin is firmly convinced that fantastic fiction can serve a didactic function.

Another important feature of Irwin's definition is his distinction between "fantasy" literature and the fantastic. A fantasy is, according to Irwin, a story founded on and controlled by an overt violation of what is normally accepted as possible; it is the narrative consequence of transforming the condition contrary to the fact itself. (Irwin 4) In a fantasy, there is no ambiguity in perception. Fantasy offers lucidity and certainty. The fantastic engages the imagination, fantasy, on the other hand, engages the intellect while creating hesitation. (Irwin 55) This means that Irwin accepts Todorov's general definition of the fantastic, but he refuses to recognize it as a separate genre.

Irwin's theory of the fantastic is problematic. If fantasy is the transformation of the condition contrary to fact into "fact" itself, it must be asked how fantasy is different from any work of fiction. Since fiction is neither fact nor contrary to fact, it is unclear how fiction accomplishes its transformation into fact. It is uncertain whether or not Irwin implies that fiction physically changes our real familiar world, or whether he means that some fiction is identical to our familiar world (and thus not fiction), whereas other fiction (fantasy) is dissimilar. It is hard to answer these questions using the theoretical formulations presented by Irwin.

A totally different approach to the fantastic can be found in Diana Waggoner's *The Hills of Faraway: A Guide to Fantasy*. Waggoner divides all fiction into four broad groups: speculative fiction, realism, post-realistic fabulation, and pre-realistic literature. She defines speculative literature in the following way:

> Speculative fiction can be briefly defined as a class of modern, "sentimental" literature that treats supernatural and/or nonexistent phenomena (such as the future) as a special class of objectively real things or events, using the low mimetic mode.[17]

Waggoner then focuses her attention on realistic literature, which explains away the supernatural as lie, coincidence or illusion. Post-realistic fabulation, she contends, is a further development of realism, whereas the pre-realistic literature does not regard the supernatural as being divorced from the rest of reality. (Waggoner 9) Waggoner divides speculative fiction into these genres: allegory, satire, utopia, imaginary voyage, traveler's tale, ghost story, fairy tale, Kunstmärchen, oriental tale, dream-story, horror story, science fiction and fantasy. (Waggoner 9)

She also points out that fantasy is distinct among the genres of speculative fiction in that it goes to the farthest extreme to establish realistic credentials for the supernatural. (Waggoner 9) Waggoner divides fantasy itself into two categories which are (1) magic in operation and (2) magic of situation. These two other categories are then in their turn divided into subcategories according to the content of the fiction, among such subcategories fairy stories, science fantasy and magic time travel can be mentioned. They all have the common component of the supernatural. Even though fantastic works are not dialectical or allegorical, they can, in Waggoner's view, be used to "enlighten and clarify." (Waggoner 9) It is interesting to note that Waggoner here, like critics such as Ostrowski and Irwin, fully acknowledges the didactic possibilities of the fantastic.

Another noteworthy theorist of the genre of the fantastic in the Anglo-Saxon world is the British novelist and critic T. E. Apter, whose study *Fantasy Literature: An Approach to Reality* (1982) exemplifies a psychological method of analysis. Apter argues from Freudian principles that the fantasist's reality is built on psychological fact.[18] A fantastic occurrence provides insight into underlying psychological concerns that disturb an apparently ordered structure. Apter thus considers fantasy anchored in reality and particularly open to psychoanalytic explication and concludes: "Psychoanalytic theory, so adept at defying absurdity, is a plausible aid to interpretation of this difficult and dubious genre." (Apter 5)

What is new in Apter's theory is the thesis that fantastic literature in fact clarifies and expands psychoanalytical theory, since the assumption is that fantasy literature exposes truth and reality.

Apter maintains that the fantastic is not a sudden intrusion into the familiar world, but rather a subtle transformation of this world, so delicate that the reader hesitates in determining the nature of the reality with which he is confronted. This critic also contrasts the marvelous, or fantasy, with the fantastic, contending that fantasy offers an escape from reality, whereas the fantastic intrudes on reality. (Apter 6) This view can be contrasted with the earlier opinion expressed by Vax, in which the fantastic is regarded as an emotional response to the unexpected, whereas fantasy is an intellectual creation. A socio-psychological aspect of the fantastic is also addressed in this analysis. Commenting on Franz Kafka's *Die Verwandlung*, Apter states:

> The fantastic circumstances can be viewed as an economic and effective means of revealing characters' interests and emotions which would be disguised or modified in surroundings well ordered by comfort or custom; in this way they would be seen to have the same purpose as the realist's plot. (Apter 1)

A German scholar, Rein Zondergeld suggests a similar socio-psychological approach to the genre of the fantastic. Zondergeld emphasizes that an important aim of fantastic literature is to expand the objective world by a dimension and to make fantasy a tool for realizing certain inner traits of the individual personality, an effort frustrated by everyday life:

> Die Phantastische Literatur hat es zu ihrer Aufgabe gemacht, die objektive Welt um eine Dimension zu erweitern, in der der Mensch durch die Macht seiner Phantasie versucht, die ihm innewohnenden Bestrebungen zur Verwirklichung seiner ganzen Persönlichkeit, welche von den strengen Gesetzen der Alltagswelt frustriert werden, Ausdruck zu verleihen.[19]

A different definition is given by another German scholar, Winfried Freund, who aspires to make the conflict between real and unreal into a structuralist dichotomy. In this definition, the real is considered "narrow" or "static," the unreal, on the other hand, is regarded as "wide" or "dynamic." Freund contends (agreeing with Caillois) that the fantastic is the unanticipated emergence of the impossible in an established and familiar world, suddenly confronted with vampires, werewolves, witches and other supernatural creatures:

> Reales und Irreales kollidieren unmittelbar. Das gänzlich Unerwartete bricht ein in eine vertraute empirische Welt und ruft Irritationen und Angst hervor, weil die herrschende Orientierung mit einem Male versagt ... Monstruöse

personale Ausprägungen des Irrealen sind beispielsweise Vampire, Werwölfe, Hexen u. ä. die bedrohend und zerstörend in die vertraute Welt einbrechen.[20]

Freund maintains that the short story is the exemplary vehicle for the fantastic, since it makes it possible for the emphasis to lie on this fantastic event, rather than losing the disruption of reality in a multitude of various plot components. (Freund 9–10)

Freund also differentiates the fantastic from fantasy by stressing that a world where something marvelous occurs as a matter of course is not fantastic, but rather fabulous:

Eine Welt, in der sich Wunderbares selbstverständlich ereignet, ist nicht fantastisch, sondern märchenhaft, da die für das Phantastische konstituive Konfrontation des Realen mit dem Irrealen hier nicht sinnfällig gemacht werden kann.[21]

Hoffmann's writings would, without a doubt, belong to the fantastic in this more restrictive sense of the word. Freund also contends, (as does for instance Zondergeld) that the fantastic has a purpose of social criticism. It is suggested that the fantastic criticizes contemporary values such as materialism and urbanization. ("Von der Aggression ...," 19). The literary function of the genre is very ambitious. Since human existence in the modern world has become so meaningless, literature must supply a new sense of meaning. ("Von der Aggression...," 29) The fantastic portrays the pointlessness of our familiar world while at the same time offering a quasi-mystical way out of this dilemma.

Jens Malte Fischer gives a definition of the fantastic which to some degree resembles that of Freund. The seemingly inconceivable occurs in the present or past, normally by means of the uncanny, the eerie, the occult etc. Fischer does not provide clear definitions of the uncanny, the eerie, or occult, and it is unclear what the seemingly inconceivable really is. But the main focus of his study appears to be an examination of individual works rather than the definition of what features these works have in common. Whereas Freund contends that the fantastic has a socio-political role, Fischer on his part assigns the genre a socio-religious role. In his opinion, the fantastic functions to some degree to replace religion, which may have become less gratifying during more secular periods of rationalism or enlightenment. (Fischer 96)

In examining the different national and analytical traditions, it becomes apparent that little overall consensus exists on significant facets of the genre of the fantastic. Problems have emerged and various perspectives have been presented because different theorists have not necessarily been discussing the same literary writings. Some theories do not reveal a comprehensive knowledge of actual works in the fantastic tradition. Moreover, most of the debate has not gone beyond the need to *define* the genre nor has it examined the more complex issues of literary quality and aesthetic principles. But there appears to be agreement on one important point: E.T.A. Hoffmann's key significance in the development of the fantastic, a matter that warrants further investigation.

Chapter Two
Elements of the Fantastic in Hoffmann's Fiction before "Die Serapionsbrüder"

Introduction

Even though E.T.A. Hoffmann was no literary theorist per se, he explicitly described the principles and techniques of his fictional works, particularly in outlining his Callot and Serapionic Principles. The Callot Principle, developed in his collection *Fantasiestücke*, advocates taking the various forms of everyday life, as they appear in the writer's inner romantic world, and representing them in a strange wonderful shimmer in which they exist. The author proceeds from the outer world of everyday life to the inner world of the imagination. In using the Serapiontic Principle, on the other hand, he proceeds from the inner world of fantasy and imagination to the outer world of reality. The ultimate goal of both principles is the same, however, since each results in a synthesis of fantasy and reality. The Callot Principle thus creates a fantastic representation of reality, whereas the Serapiontic Principle creates a realistic representation of fantasy. Both principles presuppose that the writer does not lose contact with reality.

The Serapiontic Principle was delineated in *Die Serapionsbrüder*, a frame tale containing twenty-four stories and several digressions in the form of anecdotes and essays. The work is written according to the example of Ludwig Tieck's *Phantasus* (1811), in which a group of people at a country manor read their literary productions aloud. In *Die Serapionsbrüder*, the Serapion Brotherhood, composed of Cyprian, Lothar, Ottmar, Sylvester, Theodor and Vinzenz, meets to read and discuss various narratives. The Serapionic Principle arose from Cyprian's encounter in the mountains near Bamberg with the mysterious hermit Serapion, in reality a demented count, ex-diplomat, and poet, who vanished from society and was later found dressed as a monk, preaching in the area and telling everyone that he was the martyr Serapion. He was forced to enter an insane asylum but was later released. The count continued claiming to be Serapion, telling fantastic tales and offering wisdom to anyone who would listen. When Cyprian encountered him he learned from the hermit what was later to be called the Serapion Principle in honor of this remarkable personality who told ingenious accounts of individuals full of life. This principle, which had been utilized by the brotherhood in creating their fiction, required that the brothers relate tales of fantasy and imagination as if they had actually experienced them. The narrators would not, however, retreat into a fantasy world as the count had done, but they would rather firmly anchor all their accounts in reality.

Blending the fantastic with reality is an essential trait of Hoffmann's literary achievement and a technique which the author himself regarded as novel, innovative and daring. In letters to his publisher, C. F. Kunz, he discusses the novelty of the narrative "Der goldne Topf". On January 16, 1814, for example, Hoffmann writes to Kunz: "Ich glaube Ihnen eine Gemüthergötzlichkeit zu bereiten, wenn ich ihnen anliegend die Reinschrift der ersten vier Vigilien meines Märchens sende, das ich selbst für exotisch und in der Idee neu halte."[1] A couple of months later, on March 4, 1814, Hoffmann again writes Kunz enthusiastically about the new narrative while emphasizing its literary novelty:

> Ohne Säuemnis schicke ich Ihnen in der Anlage das vollendete Märchen mit dem herzlichen Wunsche, daß es ihnen in seiner durchgehaltenen Ironie Vergnügen gewähren möge. Die Idee so das ganz Fabulose, dem aber wie ich glaube, die tiefere Deutung giebt, in das gewöhnliche Leben keck eintreten zu lassen ist allerdings gewagt und so viel ich weiß von einem teutschen Autor in diesem Maaß noch nicht benutzt worden. *(Briefwechsel 2: 445)*

Hoffmann, satisfied with his technique of combining the fantastic with everyday life in his first collection *Fantasiestücke,* makes it a prerequisite for the tales in *Die Serapionsbrüder*. In addition to formulating the Serapionic principle near the beginning of the collection and using it to create their stories, the brothers debate the principle in commenting on the narrative "Die Brautwahl." Lothar, to whom this account is attributed, calls attention to the real-life setting in which the fantastic events of his narrative occur. In the conversation that ensues the story, the difficulties of writing fantastic fiction is addressed. Theodor, generally regarded as one of the author's alter egos, remarks:

> Sonst war es üblich, ja Regel, alles, was nur Märchen hieß, ins Morgenland zu verlegen, und dabei die Märchen der Dscheherezade zum Muster zu nehmen. Die Sitten des Morgenlandes nur eben berührend, schuf man sich eine Welt, die haltlos in den Lüften schwebte und vor unsern Augen verschwamm. Deshalb gerieten aber jene Märchen meistens frostig, gleichgültig und vermochten nicht den innern Geist zu entzünden und die Fantasie aufzuregen.[2]

Such a focus on exotic characters and milieus thus risks making a story totally indifferent, lifeless and without the proper contact with the experiences of the intended reader. Instead, Theodor recommends a fantasy literature based on a clear connection between real life and fantastic events:

Ich meine, daß die Basis der Himmelsleiter, auf der man hinaufsteigen will in höhere Regionen, befestigt sein müsse im Leben, so das jeder nachzusteigen vermag. Befindet er sich dann, immer höher und höher hinaufgeklettert, in einem fantastischen Zauberreich, so wird er glauben, dies Reich gehöre auch in sein Leben hinein und sei eigentlich der wunderbar herrlichste Teil desselben. (*Werke* 7: 101–102)

This connection between reality and imagination is such a conspicuous characteristic of Hoffmann's fiction as it is reflected in most of his literary production that it elicited the following remark from Joseph Retinger, a noted French Hoffmann scholar:

Et chose curieuse, dans ses contes merveilleux même, il a toujours soin d'être réaliste. La plupart sont écrits sous l'influence d'une observation directe. Malgré son goût fantaisiste, il regard et note minutieusement tout ce qui l'entourre.[3]

Exact scrutiny of reality is one of a writer's requisites, according to a statement in one of Hoffmann's last narratives, "Des Vetters Eckfenster." The person who wishes to write fiction must, in the author's opinion, have as an initial prerequisite "an eye that really sees." This cautionary advice is given to someone who, despite lacking the ability to be a conscientious observer, intends to become a writer: "Das erste Erfordernis fehlt dir dazu, um jemals in die Fußstapfen deines würdigen lahmen Vetters zu treten, nähmlich ein Auge, welches wirklich Schaut." (*Werke* 12: 173).

Hoffmann returns to the significance of good observation several times. In a letter to the editor of the Berlin *Zuschauer,* for instance, he explains that his literary technique included looking and observing and putting down on paper what he saw, and he reiterates the absolute requirement for an author to be perceptive: "Sie wissen es nähmlich wohl schon, wie gar zu gern ich zuschaue und anschaue, und dann schwarz auf weiß von mir gebe, was ich recht lebendig erschaut." Typically, the author's most fantastic tales take place in the current mundane world. Some, such as "Der Kampf der Sänger," a medieval narrative, and "Meister Martin der Küfner und seine Gesellen," a colorful story of sixteenth-century Nuremburg, have a historical setting, but they nevertheless are based in reality and meticulously crafted in a way to make the reader accept the singular characters and the bizarre events as real.

Even though Hoffmann firmly sets most of his tales in the real world, he obscures the reality depicted in them by deliberately employing ambiguity. The reader is frequently unable to determine whether the occurrences of a tale are supernatural or factual, because the writer disapproves of narratives in which everything is explained, thereby retaining no element of mystery to fascinate the reader. Hoffmann expresses this sentiment through his alter ego Theodor, in *Die Serapionsbrüder*, immediately following the ambiguous tale "Die Automate." In this context, Theodor strongly stresses the importance of a remaining mystery for the reader:

> Nichts ist mir mehr zuwieder als wenn in einer Erzählung, in einem Roman der Boden, auf dem sich die fantastische Welt bewegt hat, zuletzt mit dem historischen so rein gekehrt wird, daß auch kein Körnchen, kein Stäubchen bleibt, wenn man so ganz abgefunden nach Hause geht, daß man gar keine Sehnsucht empfindet noch einmal hinter die Gardinen zu kucken. (*Werke* 6:113)

In his study *Le Conte fantastique en France de Nodier à Maupassant*, Pierre-Georges Castex points out that the technique of not sweeping the stage of a narrative clean, but always leaving some dust to cloud the issues is a method learned from the minor French author Jacques Cazotte, who in his work *Le Diable amoureux* (1772), suggested rational explanations for all incidents but also often reserved the possibility of supernatural explanations. (Castex 41)

In her study *"The Fantastic in the Fiction of Hoffmann and Hawthorne,"* Allienne Rimer Becker particularly underscores the direct importance of Cazotte's production for Hoffmann and also compares it to his deep admiration for Ludwig Tieck, an author from whom he also borrowed aspects of his technique. (Becker 85) Such borrowings, she asserts, are apparent in works which bear a noteworthy resemblance to Tieck's. (Becker 85) In 1815, Hoffmann even began writing a sequel to the latter's narrative "Merkwürdige Lebensgeschichte Sr. Majestät Abraham Tonelli," which he called "Neuesten Schicksale eines abendteurlichen Mannes." (Becker 87)

Hoffmann's diary also provides substantial evidence of Hoffmann's appreciation for Tieck. In a diary note from October 4, 1812, for instance, he indicates his impressions of Tieck's *Bombocciada* explaining that its narrative "Die verkehrte Welt" once again gave him poetic enthusiasm. It is also mentioned in Hoffmann's diary that he was reading "Prinz Zerbino oder die Reise nach dem guten Geschmack," Tieck's parody of popular literature of January 1813.[4]

The significant role played by Jean Paul Richter for Hoffmann's literary technique is also addressed by Becker, who emphasizes that Jean Paul directly accused Hoffmann of imitating his style. The former writer had as a favor written a preface to *Die Fantasiestücke* and had even remarked that he was responsible for the latter author's popularity in Germany. It was therefore understandable that Hoffmann chose to remove Jean Paul's preface from subsequent editions of this collection. (Becker 85–86) The editor of an English edition of Hoffmann's letters, Johanna C. Sahlin, concludes that Jean Paul and Tieck did not appreciate their disciple, who was possibly not aware of it in his modesty, had overtaken them by far.[5]

A skeptical reception, as had been the case in the reaction of some of the competitors, did not prevent the productive Hoffmann from publishing major collections of stories. The first of them was to be called *Die Fantasiestücke in Callots manier*. This collection offers some interesting examples of the author's approach to fantastic literature.

Die Fantasiestücke in Callots manier

The two initial volumes of the collection *Fantasiestücke in Callots manier* were published in Bamberg by Carl Friedrich Kunz in 1814 and contained an introduction by Jean Paul and illustrations by Hoffmann himself. A third volume appeared at the end of the same year, and a final fourth one came out in the following year. The collection was published anonymously, but with an ironic gesture Hoffmann signed two of the sketches which he drew to illustrate the tales, referring to his paradoxical behavior as "Versteckspielen," hide and seek. The author regarded the sketches as "allegorische Vignetten" On August 12, 1813, Hoffmann wrote Kunz, who had wanted an explanation of the sketches, asserting that no explanations were necessary: "Der Sinn der Allegorie in den Zeichnungen spricht sich so deutlich aus, daß ich kein Wort darüber zu sagen brauche..." (*Briefwechsel* 1:403) Two of the best known stories from *Fantasiestücke,* "Ritter Gluck" and "Der goldne Topf" lend themselves especially well to a symbolic or fantastic interpretation and can serve as examples of Hoffmann's early technique of fantastic narration.

"Ritter Gluck," the first tale in the collection, is a prime example of the writer's highly original approach to the fantastic. The story also superbly exemplifies Todorov's focus on continuing hesitation on the part of the reader as a fundamental basis for a fantastic tale where the real world is confronted by supernatural elements. This narrative indeed cleverly positions two worlds in an antithetical correlation to each other. The realistically portrayed world of Berlin in 1808 is cautiously balanced against a spiritual and supernatural world in which time or place have no meaning. A tavern in the lively Berliner Tiergarten is the environment depicted in the initial paragraphs. Since Hoffmann's objective in authoring the collection, as explained in "Jacques Callot," the introductory essay, is to produce a realistic representation of the fantastic, he incorporates in this story discussions of the Berlin musical season. In this setting, Berliners smoke, drink, debate philosophy and converse about a well-known actress, a woman whom the author may well have seen on the stage during his sojourn in Berlin in 1808.

Even though the described environment is conclusively realistic in its components, fantastic ingredients also already appear in the first paragraph of the story. The first-person narrator, sitting in a tavern, where, he explains, he likes to talk to various invisible companions about art, music and similar pleasures, suddenly notices that someone has joined him at the table. The tale becomes ambiguous at that point, since it is unclear whether or not this person is part of the real Berlin setting or just part of the imaginary world of the narrator. The world of reverie and dream appears more real to him than the world around him. He is convinced that nothing can chase away his invisible companions. This acknowledgment casts doubt on his trustworthiness as a witness to the occurrences which he reports.

The reader asks himself who this curious companion to the narrator could be. The detailed depiction of his traits, his fiery eyes, and his haggard frame make the reader believe that he is absolutely real. But the use of certain words in portraying him serves as a counterweight to the lifelike depiction and alerts the reader that he is being taken into the twilight zone of the fantastic. The following sentence, as part of the description of the mysterious companion, is typical of the author's technique:

> Das weich gerformte Kinn stand in seltsamen Kontrast mit dem geschlossenen Munde, und ein skurilles Lächeln, welches hervorbrach durch das sonderbare Muskelspiel in den eingefallenen Wagen, schien sich aufzulehnen gegen den tiefen, melancholischen Ernst, der auf der Stirn ruhte. (*Werke* 1:13).

The words "seltsam" and "sonderbar" imply that there is something curious about this person. "Ein skurilles Lächeln," a ludicrous smile, further adds to his peculiar look. Such depictions remind the reader of Jean Bellemin-Noël's emphasis on expressions such as "rires sardoniques" to define the nature of the fantastic. Later in the story the author actually also uses the word "fantastisch" to describe the enigmatic stranger.

The curious smile of the stranger is alluded to several times. He is, for example, depicted as "sonderbar lächelnd," when, at the end of the narrative, he asserts: "Ich bin der Ritter Gluck!" Hoffmann here presents a paradox. Christoph Willibald Ritter von Gluck had died in Vienna already in 1787. How could this man possibly emerge in Berlin 21 years later? No explanation is offered. The reader can, if he is so inclined, accept the supernatural apparition of the late composer and musician. The tale is completely ambiguous. Two worlds are confronted with each other; the reader as well as the narrator is caught between them and both ask themselves what is actually real.

"Ritter Gluck" includes many components to support the notion that the companion is in fact the deceased individual he claims to be. He is a first-rate musician who knows Gluck's compositions so well that he can improvise on them and further develop them. He calls Mozart his younger brother and wears old-fashioned attire under his more modern coat. In his somber room with adornments indicating past grandeur, the music paper on his piano has yellowed with age and his inkwell is in part concealed by cobwebs.

Mysteriously, the companion refers to himself as being cursed, of having abandoned what is holy, and of having to wander in Berlin, alone, isolated, not even being permitted to enter the home of someone else. He haunts music halls and opera houses constantly asking about which evil spirit has caused his predicament: "Welcher böse Geist hat mich hier festgebannt?" (*Werke* 1:20)

In "Ritter Gluck," one can detect an interesting parallel to the later tale "Der Artushof," where a peculiar artist with blank canvasses seems to be a ghost from a previous period. The spooky music performed by the Ritter Gluck is played from blank pages. The artist in the later story can disappear with the light, an ability shared by the mysterious companion in the earlier tale. Both men discover their bliss in the spiritual world of reveries and dreams.

A strictly deductive and rational explanation to the events in this narrative would suggest that the bizarre musician is either intoxicated or deranged. There is support in the story for either of these interpretations. The strange performer loves his wine. As soon as one bottle is empty, he eagerly uncorks another. His deformed physical traits imply lunacy. His general grotesqueness makes him socially odd or peculiar. He is, to a great extent, a caricature of a musician. Moreover, his utterances regarding his being in the kingdom of dreams could be interpreted as the rambling of a lunatic. He confesses to seeing, hearing and feeling things which others do not.

The closing part of the tale suggests that the companion is insane, since he gives the narrator a copy of Gluck's *Armida*, which proves to be music paper without a single note on it. He has the narrator turn the pages of this blank score while he performs the music. A lucid mind would thus consider him deranged.

There is a noteworthy similarity between this curious man and one of the characters in the later collection *Die Serapionsbrüder*, namely the eccentric who professes to be the martyr Serapion. Both, filled with burning creative imagination, contend that they are something quite implausible, persons who are known to be dead. They are artistic personalities. In moments of cosmic consciousness, the man who refers to himself as Ritter Gluck enters into a transcendental sphere of reality in which his intellect is enlarged and he becomes an artistic master.

Yet another interpretation of the narrative is conceivable. The curious musician can simply be considered the product of the narrator's imagination. Already at the beginning of the story, the narrator states that he likes reveries on art and music in which he converses with invisible companions whom nothing can dispel. The companion, seen in this light, becomes the double or Doppelgänger of the narrator. He communicates what the narrator himself wishes to suppress.

An example of this can be found in the initial conversation between the two men when the companion addresses the question about the narrator's profession:

"Sie sind Musiker und Kenner von Profession ...." (*Werke* 1:13) The narrator contradicts this, but the companion insists, asking if the narrator has never composed. The latter at this point confesses to being interested in music and has composed, but he has abandoned this activity since he perceived his own compositions as dull and uninspired: "Ja, ich habe mich in der Kunst versucht; nun fand ich alles, was ich, wie es mich dünkte, in Augenblicken der Begeisterung geschrieben hatte, nachher matt und langweilig; da ließ ich's denn bleiben." (*Werke* 1:16) The narrator thus clearly regards himself as a failed composer. The companion, however, scolds him for abandoning his music.

The author had indeed a sense of inadequacy as a musician at the time of writing "Ritter Gluck." Grave financial problems reinforced this pessimistic sentiment. In a letter to his old friend Hippel, dated May 7, 1808, Hoffmann admits to having very little to eat. He has, he explains, only eaten a little bit of bread during five days. (*Briewechsel* 1:242) It was under such circumstances that the author began writing his story. On October 26, he had to resign his post of Kapellmeister with the Bamberg Orchestra, which was dissatisfied with his performance. On January 12, 1809, he sent "Ritter Gluck" to his publisher.

These setbacks in the author's life give some credence to the notion that this story in some ways represents the narrator's wish to actually *be* Ritter Gluck. The belief that the companion may be the imagined Doppelgänger of the narrator also leads to another theory. Perhaps it is the narrator who is deranged or has imbibed far too much wine. It could be equally possible that the narrator hallucinates or suffers from alcoholic delirium.

An additional interpretation of the story, offered by Jean Ricci, suggests that "Ritter Gluck" could be regarded as depicting the education of a musician. ("Le fantastique ...," 15) Whatever interpretation the reader adopts, the tale is rich with the multifaceted perspectives of the Romantic ironist. There is a constant ironic reflection of thoughts and ideas. The bizarre companion often appears with a strange smile upon his face. His suggested lunacy gives him a fateful quality, and yet he is so utterly absurd as to be almost amusing. Allienne Rimer Becker describes the impact of the story in this way: "By making his story completely ambiguous, and by the use of Romantic irony and the grotesque, Hoffmann has created with this, his first tale, a masterpiece of fantastic literature." (Becker 103)

"Ritter Gluck" can most definitely be regarded as a classical example of a story which fits Todorov's definition of the "pure" fantastic very well. No solution as to the identity of the mysterious musician is ever offered in the story. The reader's hesitation with regards to the true nature of the tale remains unchanged to the very end. With this structure, the narrative becomes the first in a long series of accounts of this kind penned by Hoffmann.

In another story from *Fantasiestücke*, "Der goldne Topf," Todorov's analysis could be applicable in the same way, since this story too is firmly based on the notion of the hesitation and outright amazement of the reader. In this tale, Hoffmann develops and uses Romantic irony, the grotesque and ambiguity to build the fantastic structure of the narrative. He establishes irony in this tale as "a fully developed literary principle," in the words of Robert Mollenauer, who maintains that the irony of the work originates in the painful awareness of the duality of life. Diana Stone Peters draws a similar conclusion when she underscores the importance of irony as a structural principle. In other words, Hoffmann employs irony as a principle of structure in order to grasp and resolve the essentially dualistic nature of the universe.[6]

The author not only utilizes irony as a principle of structure in the story, but he also manipulates it by playing considerably with the point-of-view of the narrative, producing a mosaic with several perspectives, including (1) a change from third- to first-person narrator, (2) a letter written by one of the protagonists to the author, (3) an embedded narrative structure. By switching to first-person narration, as Becker points out, the writer intrudes into the account, complaining, as a typical romantic ironist, of his inability to write a conclusion to the tale. (Becker 104) In the letter, one of the protagonists offers to supply information and help in completing the narrative. The author describes how he responded to the letter by visiting the character, the Archivarius Lindhorst, who served him a beverage in a golden goblet. The Archivarius explained to Hoffmann that this was the favorite beverage of Johannes Kreisler. The allusion to Kreisler, who appears in other stories by Hoffmann as a self-portrait, is playfully ironic. The technique of the author entering the tale as a character was a technique sometimes used by romantic ironists.

"Der goldne Topf" is replete with such irony and it is upheld throughout the account by the consistent doubling of occurrences and individuals in the confrontation which appears between the everyday world of common middle-class life and the bizarre dreams and visions of the protagonists. Dresden, with its well-known landmarks, is the chosen environment in which the tale takes place, opening on Ascension Day as the student Anselmus runs through the Old Black Gate of the City. The characters of the narrative dine, imbibe, smoke and enjoy the bourgeois life of the city, which is counterbalanced, by a series of fantastic occurrences.

The tale itself is mirrored in the embedded story about the dragon Phosphoros and the fire-lily serpents, which parallels the primary account and illustrates it symbolically. The utilization of a story within a story, a manifestation of Romantic irony, is a technique which the author learned from reading Tieck's "Der gestiefelte Kater," a play which he strongly admired.

The characters of the tale have their mirror reflections. One could consider Anselmus the psychic double of Register Heerbrand, or perhaps rather a projection of the latter character since he vanishes when Heerbrand marries Veronika, ending his need to live in the world of fantasy. It could be concluded that Anselmus simply embodies the unconscious mind, whereas Heerbrand represents the conscious mind of the same character. Serpentina, the green serpent whom Anselmus marries, is at times identified with Veronika. Other characters also have dual identities. One example is Lindhorst, Serpentina's father, who is the psychic double of Dean Paulmann, Veronika's father.

The psychic doubles of Heerbrand, Veronika and Paul, as if reflected in a mirror, constitute contrastive images of these individuals. In their doubles the rational, customary and typical everyday characters are mysterious, irrational and peculiar. A synthesis of the two polarities seen in these characters gives, as Becker especially stresses, a transcendental picture of reality that the Romantic ironist attempts to achieve. (Becker 106) Irrespective of whether or not the characters are "doubled," it is normal for Hoffmann to treat his literary personalities in an ironic way. Peter von Matt addresses this aspect of the author's technique by pointing out that it is one of the most important characteristics of his authorship: "Es ist eines der bedeutendsten Characteristica der Hoffmannschen Erzählungen, daß von wenigen Ausnahmen abgesehen, alle Helden ständig ironisiert werden."[7]

The depiction of the ridiculous and grotesque Anselmus is a prime example of the author's usual irony. The story derides the gawky young man who knocks over the goods of the old woman and who loses his hair-piece when bowing to impress the councillor. At the conclusion of the tale, the irony is escalated when the student, repudiating a cozy middle-class life with a good position and a domestic spouse, abandons the world of reality to live in a mythical Atlantis with an imaginary mate. Had Anselmus fallen for the attraction of Veronika and a comfortable middle-class lifestyle, he would have lost his own identity. Looked upon in this fashion, the tale has traditionally (as exemplified by Harvey Hewett-Thayer's biography of the author) been regarded as an allegory of the existence of the artist.[8]

Anselmus is not alone in being a grotesque personality. The characters of Serpentina, Liese and Lindhorst are also clearly grotesque. The bizarre combination of flora, fauna and human elements produces a disorganized and truly fantastic atmosphere. Unreal images are conveyed especially through peculiar blending found in the fanciful depictions of nature: the flowers in Lindhorst's garden are insects and birds. Lilies are snakes, snakes are lilies, etc.

Ambiguity is blended with the grotesque and ironic components to make the tone and environment of the story fantastic. Inconceivable occurrences appear to take place, such as the young student's vision of the golden serpents. Anselmus and the others do, however, hesitate regarding the authenticity of these curious events. The visions could be a consequence of sickness, insanity, drunkenness or mesmerism. The story lends credence to all those explanations, but mesmerism appears to be a major factor since components such as Serpentina's blue eyes, Lindhorst's shining ring and the shining almost seductive quality of the pot itself are hinted at when fantastic occurrences are described. Considering the author's strong interest in hypnotism, Lindhorst's control over Anselmus could be regarded as hypnotic suggestion.

It is problematic to decide what is actually happening in the narrative since the language of the account often implies, without definite substantiation, that some peculiar or supernatural occurrence takes place. Phrases such as "Es schien ...," "Es war wie ...," and "Er glaubte . . .," exemplify the consciously ambiguous formulations in "Der goldne Topf."

The dream components of the story also make the account ambiguous and mirror the real world in an ironic way. It is, however, hard to ascertain what is a dream and what is not, since the dream may be the double of familiar reality in the same way as Serpentina serves as a double of Veronika. Fantastic dreams are an important element in the tale (as in much of the author's work). In a letter to Kunz, dated March 24, 1814, Hoffmann confirms the importance of dreams as a background to his literary production (even though he specifically refers to another story in this context) and he concludes with a mythological reference: "Oneiros, der Traumgott hat mir einen Roman inspiriert, der in lichten Farben, in dem Tom I. beynahe vollendet. Das Büchlein heißt die Elexiere des Teufels" (*Briefwechsel* 2:454)

In the tales of Hoffmann, as Inge Stegman underscores in the essay "Die Wirklichkeit des Traumes bei E.T.A. Hoffmann," dreams serve as a mirror of higher reality which the waking consciousness is unable destroy. Since Hoffmann employed the dream component in a story so frequently, the utilization of fantastic dreams in fiction, can at least to some extent be traced to him.

One example of the importance of the dream element in "Der goldne Topf" can be found in the seventh Vigil where the author intentionally confuses the world of dreams with that of waking reality. Veronika wakes up in her room one morning, wondering if she has dreamed or has actually experienced the terrifying occurrences of the previous night. Her bizarre meeting with the old witch has the character of a strange dream, or perhaps rather that of an outright nightmare. In the middle of the action, the author intrudes into the story, thereby breaking the illusion which he has created, asserting that if the reader had stumbled across the witch and the girl in the field this night, the spell would have been broken by his intrusion and the witch would have disappeared. After having destroyed the atmosphere and tone, the author brings the depicted scene back.

Most of the fantastic sequences in the narrative are not, however, dreams or nightmares, but rather visions of unexplained ambiguous origin, which allow the reader to determine whether they are created by supernatural forces, or induced by hypnosis, intoxicants, or some other means. The visions have the same purpose as the dreams, exposing a fantastic universe divided in two.

The grotesque juxtaposition of contradictory and sometimes even ludicrous components adds humor to the account. There is unquestionably much grotesque humor in the story that clearly originates in the absurd and incongruous demeanor of the author's characters, as is already apparent at the beginning of the tale, when Anselmus clumsily runs into the basket filled with apples and cookies. This bizarre beginning of story is furthermore an excellent illustration of Thomas Cramer's brief definition of the grotesque in its relation to humor (following Wolfgang Kayser's theories on the subject) in his study *Das Groteske bei E.T.A. Hoffmann*: ". . . die Komik ist umgeschlagen, nicht mehr der Mensch beherrscht die Komik, sondern die Komik beherrscht den Menschen." Anselmus clearly typifies this definition.

Genuine madness also becomes a major aspect of the nature of Hoffmann's humor. This madness emanates from the antithesis between the dreams and visions of Hoffmann's characters and the normal reality in which they live. The author himself recognized this contrast as the true origin of his humor; he even directly referred to this connection in a testimony written in his own defense in a libel suit which had arisen surrounding his narrative "Meister Floh" by stating:

> Der Kontrast einer inneren Gemütsstimmung mit den Situationen des Lebens is eine Grundbasis des Komischen, welches in dem Märchen vorherrschen sollte, und so glaubte ich die Erfindung nach bewährten Theorien für glücklich halten zu dürfen. (*Briefwechsel* 3:258)

Hoffmann moreover explained, in his defense, that the humorous author must be allowed to move freely and cheerfully in his fantastic world: "Dem humoristischen Dichter muβ es freistehen, sich in dem Gebiet seiner phantastischen Welt frei und frisch zu bewegen." (*Briefwechsel* 3:260) He concluded that he freely followed the flight of his imagination as the story warranted, thereby humorously reflecting the images of the real world as if caught in a mirror. (*Briefwechsel* 3:262) Humor is one element that is particularly striking in "Der goldne Topf." The story is one of the author's most famous tales and it contains an original and adroit blend of components based on both fantasy and reality. Romantic irony is used as a principle of structure to resolve the polarities which are created by the presence of dreams, visions, intoxicants, hypnosis and ambiguity of language.

The grotesque, contributing to the fantastic effect of the narrative by its ridiculous, incongruous, bizarre and frequently humorous juxtapositions, adds an ominous element, since the strange occurrences and individuals are sometimes entirely out of control in a chaotic universe. The fantastic events of the tale are set against the realistic middle-class life of Dresden in the early nineteenth century. "Der goldne Topf" typifies the techniques which were to make Hoffmann famous. The collection in which the story was published, *Fantasiestücke*, was to be followed several years later by a second group of stories, gathered under the name *Die Nachtstücke*.

Die Nachtstücke

Hoffmann's second collection of short fiction, *Die Nachtstücke* was published in two volumes in 1816–17. Just as he had found inspiration for the *Fantasiestücke* in the art of Jacques Callot, he was inspired by baroque paintings for *Die Nachtstücke*, whose title is symbolically revealing. In this type of painting, darkness dominates the picture, with the only light coming from moonlight, which is reflected in the light of the sun, or from artificial sources, such as candles, lanterns, or fires. In choosing this title for the tales which make up the two volumes of stories, Hoffmann indicated that they would be accounts in which the darkness of life predominates.

The first story of the collection, entitled "Der Sandmann," is an excellent example of the further development of Hoffmann's approach to the genre of the fantastic. With its deliberate narrative ambiguity from beginning to end it also fits perfectly into Todorov's model for an analysis of the fantastic. "Der Sandmann" is a tale composed, like the other narratives, of components of romantic irony, the grotesque, and ambiguity. The author, frequently haunted by weird horrors and apparitions, expressed in this story the very darkness he felt, or to use his own expression, the devil thrust his tail into every part of the story. The arabesque structure of the tale is the exterior formal expression of the paradoxical and ironic interior characteristics of the account. It contains essentially two perspectives, that of the artist Nathanael and that of his fiancee Clara. Nathanael's assertion that dark demonic powers make a puppet of man has its counterweight in Clara's contention that the darkness exists exclusively in man's mind and can be eliminated by an act of the will. In the letters which he writes to his fiancee and her brother Lothar, Nathanael claims that he is plagued by sinister forces. In her response, Clara expresses her view that a stable mind can get rid of such evil elements. An omniscient narrator who does not side with either Clara or Nathanael closes the story by informing the reader about what becomes of them. The reader must then piece the tale together from the two letters of Nathanael, Clara's letter, and the report of the third-person narrator.

One particularly absurd event in the story is Nathanael's falling in love with an automaton, Olimpia, a robot-like contraption whom he believes to be a sympathetic and loving woman. At the same time Nathanael considers Clara a wooden doll. When he contemplates marrying Olimpia, the smile which appears on the face of Professor Spalazani, Olimpia's "father," is a typical Hoffmann touch revealing the irony of the circumstance. When Nathanael ultimately becomes aware of the truth about the automaton, he is no longer able to write. Since the only one who appreciates his literary production is a lifeless doll, he no longer has any place in society. As a result he goes insane and commits suicide.

The narrator interrupts this somber tale of insanity and death to ponder humorously the way he wrote the account and how others reacted to these events. With a clear change in tone, he jests ironically with phrases such as "Günstiger

Leser!" and "O mein Leser!" Having concluded that the tale lacks humor, he then interrupts the story to facetiously contemplate the legal ramifications of duping society by making people believe that a doll is a human being. The ironic purpose of these humorous interruptions is quite evident.

Further examples of Romantic irony are found, as has been stressed by among others Hermann August Korff in his study *Geist der Goethezeit*, in the portrayal of the characters themselves. The author plays with his characters, making them the toys of fate, but at the same time having their fate be the consequence of their personality. Nathanael, for instance, has the features of a caricature of an author. He is incapable of understanding the ironic point of view, an attitude which would have helped him transcend his situation and ultimately to survive. Had Nathanael been a real romantic author, instead of just a caricature, he would have had a healthy distance to what he had written as well as a more ambivalent attitude towards life.

Another aspect of the ironic elements used in the narrative is the existence of doubles. The nursemaid who puts the fear of the sandman into the child Nathanael is the reverse image of his mother. These two characters could be regarded, as has been suggested by Robert Mühlher, as the "good" and the "bad" mother-figures of the story.[9] The "bad" mother tells the little boy the sandman story, which parallels occurrences in Nathanael's life. With the nursemaid's story, the grotesque enters the narrative. Nathanael's head is filled with visions of an evil sandman who snatches away the bloody eyes of children to take home to feed his own offspring.

The protagonist, after having heard this horrifying tale, comes to identify Coppelius, a far from attractive man who makes nocturnal visits to the family home, with the sandman. Coppelius has green feline eyes, a hooked nose and hideous hairy hands. Especially his demonic laugh convinces the boy that he is a person of transcendental evil. Nathanael describes in his letter to his fiancée how even his own father takes on the same grotesque appearance as Coppelius while working with him on an obscure project. The protagonist portrays his father's transformation in this way: "Ein gräßlicher kramphafter Schmerz schien seine sanften ehrlichen Züge zum häßlichen widerwertigen Teufelsbilde verzogen zu haben. Er sah dem Coppelius ähnlich." (*Werke* 3:9)

The grotesque appearance of Coppelius is but one instance of grotesque elements in the story. The protagonist's incredible relation to Olimpia is another obvious example. The bizarre situation in which Nathanael sees Olimpia at a time when she has black holes where her eyes have been seems particularly grotesque. On the floor two eyes lie staring at him. The significance of these eyes should, as Ulrich Hohoff also has pointed out in his study of the tale, be seen in the context of the old image of the eyes as mirrors of the soul. This combination of the human and the machine is fantastic. It is also inexplicable. Such components in the story-line unquestionably contribute to the character of the tale as a depiction of something utterly fantastic and irrational.

Even though no lucid or rational explanation is given in the story for the curious occurrences leading up to the death of the protagonist, literary critics have aspired to provide one, although Hoffmann has intentionally written an ambiguous tale. One classic example is Sigmund Freud who alleges that "Der Sandmann" is a case history of a "castration complex" since the fear of blindness could be considered an "Ersatz" for a fear of castration. Freud concludes:

> Wie psychologisch richtig es aber ist, daß der durch den Kastrationskomplex an den Vater fixierte Jüngling der Liebe zur Weibe unfähig wird, zeigen zahlreiche Krankenanalysen, deren Inhalt zwar weniger phantastisch, aber kaum minder traurig ist als die Geschichte des Studenten Nathanael.[10]

It is interesting to note that Freud, by contending that Nathanael's problem is all in his head, wholeheartedly sides with Clara.

Some critics take the view of the protagonist, however, and believe that the demonic powers which torment Nathanael are authentic. Robert Mühlher, for instance, belongs to this camp. (Mühlher 66) Harvey Hewett-Thayer agrees, and asserts that Hoffmann would not acknowledge any rational explanation of Coppelius and his power over Nathanael. (Hewett-Thayer 188) For another scholar, Johannes Klein, the protagonist is a typical individual of his time who is driven into the demonic by technology.[11]

A critic like Charles Hayes contends that the text does not justify supporting either the view of Nathanael or Clara. Hayes considers Hoffmann's dreamers the first "dropouts" from bourgeois society. He also writes:

> Weder die eine noch die andere Interpretation läßt sich vom Text her rechtfertigen. Nathanaels unglückliches Ende ist ein höchst stilisiertes literarisches Ereignis und entspricht in keiner Weise dem, was ein wirklicher Mensch erlebt haben könnte. (Hayes 186)

Hayes' comment that Nathanael's demise is a highly stylized literary event and does not correspond in any way to what a real person could have experienced leads to a consideration of the symbolic components of the tale, which can easily be misunderstood, especially keeping the deliberate ironic ambivalence of the narrative in mind. This ambivalence is quite clear particularly in the portrayal of the characters. One important example of this technique is, as Allianne Becker has pointed out, Clara with her ironic smile who could be regarded as a caricature of the Enlightenment; even her name is almost a pun on the word "Aufklärung." (Becker 149) Clara is a classicist, whereas Nathanael is a romanticist.

The romantic point of view strongly emphasizes the importance of symbolism, also in portrayal of characters. The grotesque and satanic Coppelius, rather than being a real person, could be regarded as a symbolic representation of evil. His demonic laughter, like his dark and annihilating humor ultimately destroys the protagonist.

Nathanael's loss of his eyes is of key significance since, as Becker also notes, it means that he loses his creative vision. (Becker 150) Without eyes he is unable to synthesize his inner world of vision with the exterior world of society, because, as observed by Günther Hartung in his essay on "Der Sandmann," the eyes are where the outer and inner worlds coalesce.[12]

The elements of irony, the grotesque, and ambiguity have created a masterpiece of fantastic fiction as well as one of Hoffmann's best known works. Its structure and general themes resemble several of the other tales in the collection and share their suitability as examples of the Todorovian "pure" fantastic. Similar components would prove to be of key importance also in the author's third collection of stories, which was to be entitled *Die Serapionsbrüder*.

Chapter Three
The Role of the Frames in "Die Serapionsbrüder"

The frame (including the subframes of the different volumes) in the collection *Die Serapionsbrüder* are of substantial importance for the interpretation of the inner stories themselves. But in the hands of most critics, as Vickie Ziegler has pointed out in her study *Bending the Frame in the German Cyclical Narrative*, the frame has suffered the fate of delinquent relatives in a respectable family. Ziegler also underscores the fact that like those unfortunate brothers sisters and cousins whose presence raises awkward moments, the frame has been misunderstood, castigated, and, in many instances, disowned outright and cast out. (Ziegler 117) Possibly the most negative judgment of the frame in the collection,—completely dismissing it—has been made by Hans von Müller. In a discussion originally published in *Zeitschrift für Bücherfreunde* regarding the frame of *Die Serapionsbrüder* as a whole, as well as the individual frames of the different volumes, von Müller chooses to ignore the frame structure when outlining the structure of the collection.[1]

Some individual tales, such as "Rat Krespel," "Das Fräulein von Scuderi" and "Die Bergwerke zu Falun" have attracted critical praise and interpretation, but the only part of the frame which has until recently received much notice has the been the *Serapionsprinzip*, as exemplified in Ilse Winter's study on the subject. In his biography, *E.T.A. Hoffmann oder die Tiefe zwischen Stern und Erde: eine Biographie*, Eckhart Kleßmann gives a more positive assessment of the work as a whole, *including* the frame. Kleßmann concludes that the collection must be regarded as a unique and unified work since it includes in consolidated form chief components of Hoffmann's art and, as a result of this, also his world view:

> Was aber bleibt, ist der mächtige Gesamteindruck, der Gelungenes und nicht ganz so Gelungenes zur Einheit verschmilzt und die äußeren Bedingungen des Entstehens vergessen läßt. Daß die Grundkonzeption der *Serapions-brüder* und ihr künstlicher Ertrag homogen wirken, zeugt für die Geschlossenheit und Festigkeit von Hoffmanns Weltbild und Ästhetik und zeugt für die Kraft der hier enthaltenen großen Erzählungen, die das weniger Bedeutende in den Hintergrund rücken und vergessen machen.[2]

A positive appraisal of the work as a whole (including the frame) is also typical of Lothar Pikulik's study *E.T.A. Hoffmann als Erzähler: Ein Kommentar zu den "Serapionsbrüdern"*. This study gives the reader comprehensive background information and a brief summary of each tale and includes comments on predominant themes and valuable interpretations of individual works. The study does not, however, deal with the interaction between the frame and inner narratives as a continuous web. Whereas Pikulik gives a helpful general introduction to the frame, he does not treat in detail the correspondences between the frame and the inner stories.[3]

The frame of *Die Serapionsbrüder* deserves particular attention, as Ziegler has rightly emphasized, due to its singular position among the author's works and within Romanticism. (Ziegler 118) One of the major benefits of the frame is that it offers a special perspective of a theoretical debate on ideas such as the role of madness in the development of the artist and the nature of the artist's relationship to life, directly juxtaposed with accounts which address these issues. While the author at times included such discussions of ideas and theories in narratives such as "Der Magnetiseur" and "Der Dichter und Komponist," nowhere else in his literary production does he offer such a comprehensive discussion of concepts of key importance for his thought. The frame furthermore presents critical judgments on his own and other authors' fiction.

The purpose of the frame is in part that of a repository of information on a great assortment of subjects and it moreover supplies a wall of protection against menacing exterior forces, such as the uncanny might of the *Magnetiseur* or the omnipresent danger of insanity. One scholar, Horst Conrad, has made the observation that Hoffmann enjoys juxtaposing peculiar occurrences with the sentiments of educated people, a tendency which, according to Conrad, leaves the reader suspended between logic and the irrational.[4]

The vivid discussions on the nature of reality and the irrational in the circle of confidants called "Die Serapionsbrüder," whether they are composites of the author's friends or first and foremost alter egos, give the frame characters the opportunity to debate disturbing or complicated issues in a safe environment. This method provides a certain necessary distance from the problems debated. The inner accounts which address topics approached in the frame provide the opportunity to explore the subject or difficulties in ways which give the emotions expression which a rational debate is unable to do, and nevertheless the fictional character of the tales assists in keeping the questions involved at a comfortable distance.

All the above factors motivate a brief analysis of the thematic correspondences between the frame and the inner narratives, as well as other intricate relations on different levels which exist between inner and outer tales. Such an analysis will reveal an unexpected unity in the collection as well as shed new light on the individual accounts themselves.

It is interesting to note what Hoffmann himself has to say about the unity of, and interrelations within, the work. One of the main arguments against a sincere consideration of the frame has been the author's seemingly nonchalant outlook on it, as demonstrated in his negotiations with his publisher Georg Reimer.

In a letter dated February 17, 1818, written in response to a previous note by Reimer, the author agrees to the latter's proposals regarding a collection of short fiction, discusses the tales to be included, and then asks for advice. In the same letter, he complains about the difficulties in finding a good name for the collection:

"Es hat aber daran gelegen, daß mir bis jetzt noch kein vernünftiger Titel ... eingefallen ist." (*Briefwechsel* 2:156)

Harvey Hewett-Thayer is probably right in his study *Hoffmann: Author of the Tales*, when he assumes that the success of *Fantasiestücke* and *Nachtstücke* must have strongly tempted Reimer to directly request another collection. (Hewett-Thayer 101) The letter also demonstrates that Hoffmann's plans were still unspecific. He appears to have thought in terms of only one single volume. Not until the succeeding summer did the author and his publisher decide (at least in writing) to publish a second.

Apart from the admittedly slowly evolving planning of the collection, it has also sometimes been contended (for instance by René Wellek) that the frame is simply an external apparatus which is intended to bring together stories published independently and therefore does not distinguish the stories in *Die Serapionsbrüder* from stories collected without any framework. Wellek thus implies that the tales were published before the author had written the frame. This assumption is, however, only to some degree correct.

This idea of a succeeding "rationalization" of already produced material has been significant in many interpretations of the frame. But it is important to remember, as Ziegler has correctly stressed, that only eleven out of twenty-six pieces included in the collection had been written before the author began the frame for the first volume. (Ziegler 120) Considering the fact that the majority of the material was produced when Hoffmann was composing the frame, the possibility should at least be admitted that some of the same themes which found their expression in the individual accounts may also have appeared in the frame. It is worth observing that in a letter, Hoffmann seems proud of the fact that he is bringing new material into the collection. He states that the fourth volume, with a few exceptions, contains only new tales. (*Briefwechsel* 2:269) Moreover, the tales in the third and fourth volumes, except "Erscheinungen," were written concurrently with the frame. The frame constitutes about a sixth of the total text, a fact which would indicate that the author indeed paid serious attention to it. Considering this background, it is very easy to agree with Ziegler's conclusion that Hoffmann would not have used either the time or the energy to write so much about difficult issues in the frame if its existence had only a purely financial motivation. (Ziegler 121)

Apart from the indisputable fact that much of the material had been previously published, the status of the frame has not necessarily been elevated by another aspect of common approaches to it, namely the elements of biography that surround it. In the attempt to identify the *Serapionsbrüder* issues of literary qualities have been largely neglected, since the frame, in the opinion of several scholars, was demoted to a thinly concealed depiction of the *Seraphinerorden*. This company of literary colleagues began to meet once a week after the author's arrival in Berlin in the fall of 1814. Among the members of the circle were Hoffmann's friend and biographer Julius Edward Hitzig, Friedrich de la Motte Fouqué, Carl Wilhelm Contessa, Adalbert von Chamisso and Johann Ferdinand Koreff. The formal name of the group came from a liturgical calendar which commemorated the martyr

Serapion Sindontina. In an essay on the group, Friedrich Schnapp mentions that the circle met until sometime in the spring of 1820. Hoffmann was hard at work at the frame during this period.

Numerous efforts have been made to identify the six *Serapionsbrüder*, Theodor, Cyprian, Ottmar, Lothar, Vinzenz and Sylvester in the frame with members of the *Seraphinerorden/Serapion* circle. But many scholars also deliberately avoid matching individual characters with the author and his acquaintances. It is well known that Hoffmann brought most of his friends into his literary production in different ways. But, as Wulf Segebrecht has pointed out in his study *Autobiographie und Dichtung: Eine Studie zum Werk E.T.A. Hoffmanns*, this hardly motivates taking a character in a frame that is the creation of the author and matching him directly with a historical person. Events come into the author's fantastic and often humorous focus and his descriptions may remind the reader at least superficially of one of his acquaintances; then Hoffmann takes the opposite side of the issue, emphasizing that different characters are only different sides of himself. This is a thought process which is reflected also in the writer's diary in a note from November 6, 1809, where he states: "Ich denke mir mein Ich durch ein Vervielfältigungsglas - alle Gestalten die sich um mich herum bewegen sind Ichs und ich ärgere mich über ihr tun und lassen." (*Tagebücher* 107) This well-known excerpt appears to motivate a substantial degree of wariness on the part of the scholar in the clearly perilous domain of oversimplified biographically inspired conjectures.

It is, as the above quote implies, possible to see the six *Serapionsbrüder* as different manifestations of the author himself. But it is probably more beneficial to see the characters in relation to a somewhat abstract figure, i.e. the artist in general and his encounters with the seen and unseen world, with exterior reality and interior vision and its artistic presentation. Such confrontations appear already early in the frame with the appearance of the insane count who seriously believes that he is the Christian martyr Serapion wandering around the desert outside Alexandria and Thebe. The author, who wrote the narrative about Serapion to motivate the choice of the name day, consolidated in that tale and the following frame debate numerous of his most deeply held convictions regarding art and reality. For that reason, the character of Serapion is of key importance for the understanding of frame-inner story relationships.

Various groups of critics have approached Serapion's role in very different ways. One group considers Serapion as a clearly positive model for the writer. This is exemplified by Peter von Matt who considers congeniality ("Gemütlichkeit") a dominating theme of the frame and tries to integrate the Serapion into it. Von Matt in fact perceives this figure to be a model for the ideal artist.[5]

Another view is to regard Serapion as an important but imperfect character. Lothar's comments on Serapion's temperament in the frame would give credence to such an interpretation. While he believes that Serapion was a genuine poet, since he actually had seen what he had announced, he also depicts the count's insanity as the consequence of a lack of sense of reality that gives us entrance into an inner spiritual world. (*Werke* 5: 60–61)   The authentic artist must attempt to attain a synthesis of the outer world and the inner metaphysical one. Serapion has some of the traits of a real poet, but, since he does not acknowledge the existence of an outside reality, he is unable to serve as an entirely positive model for the author in the frame. Even though Serapion has many characteristics of a natural poet, his stories are never directly related. He is incapable of understanding the dualism ("Duplizität") of existence, which presupposes terrestrial physical reality. Serapion can never make the narrative principle which bears his name evolve, since he is not aware of this dualism. The *Serapionsbrüder* will instead have to do it for him.

Serapion's madness clouds and garbles the borderline between real and unreal to such a degree that appraisal and examination of the true nature of reality ultimately become inconceivable. One scholar, Siegfried Schumm, maintains in his study *Einsicht und Darstellung* that this mental condition disqualifies Serapion as an ideal, since contrary to the members of the Serapion Circle, he is unable to accept criticism. Schumm mentions the example of the insane Count's belief that when he sees the towers of B he is convinced that they are the skyline of Alexandria. A disagreement would upset his equilibrium. Nevertheless, precisely in this unstable state of mind, Serapion, as Friedrich Auhuber proposes in his study *In einem fernen dunklen Spiegel: E.T.A. Hoffmanns Poetisierung der Medizin*, embodies the openness of the Serapion Circle to eccentrics and outsiders, in order to illustrate the intricate and inevitable intertwining of the natural everyday existence with the netherworld of dark forces.[6]

A disturbing state which confirms the unclear boundaries between the sane and the insane comes across in the conversation between Serapion and Cyprian, in which Serapion proves to his own satisfaction that Cyprian, not he, requires the assistance of a physician. The location of the Serapion story in the introduction to *Die Serapionsbrüder* emphasizes the significance of the connection of insanity with intensified perception and understanding and its definite benefit for the creative artist. Cyprian, the figure in the frame perhaps most fascinated by abnormal mental conditions, motivates this interest by contending that his relations with deranged individuals has activated and reinforced his own mind:

> ...immer glaube ich, daß die Natur gerade beim Abnormen Blicke vergönne in ihre schauerlichste Tiefe, und in der Tat, selbst in dem Grauen, das mich oft bei jenem seltsamen Verkehr befing, gingen mir Ahnungen und Bilder auf, die meinen Geist zum besonderen Aufschwung stärkten und belebten. (*Werke* 5: 29–30)

There are two primary reasons for this preoccupation with insanity: revelation of the inner depths of nature, and the stimulus such revelations have to offer the artist. As a result of this, Serapion, who has an artistic vision, must be at least to some extent insane. His madness is both a prerequisite for and warning to the artist; as a result, insanity becomes a significant element in the stories of the collection.

Arresting examples of individuals with artistic sensitivities who are threatened by insanity appear near the beginning and the end of the frame (Serapion, Rat

Krespel and Zacharias Werner). Other artistic people in the inner tales are directly menaced by dementia, as for instance Heinrich von Ofterdingen in "Der Kampf der Sänger," Berklinger in "Der Artushof" and Cardillac in "Das Fräulein von Scuderi." Persons who are not artistic but whose personalities are assaulted by exterior powers which transform their mental condition include Fredinand in "Die Automate," Elis Fröbom in "Die Bergwerke zu Falun," Angelika in "Der unheimliche Gast," Marie in "Nußknacker und Mäusekönig" and Graf Hyppolit in "Eine Vampirgeschichte." Apart from these characters from the inner narratives, there are many instances in the frame of victims of insanity and psychic powers.

It is thus abundantly clear that madness is a major theme in *Die Serapionsbrüder* which sometimes tends to dominate over other "subthemes." Hoffmann's diary offers evidence of the author's own concern with his mental condition. In an entry from January 5, 1811, he asks himself why he thinks about madness much of the time: "Warum denke ich schlafend und wachend so oft an den Wahnsinn?—Ich meine, geistige Ausleerungen könnten wie ein Aderlaß wirken." (*Tagebücher* 112) Robert Mühlher concludes that part of the author's concerns about his mental state arose as a result of the fact that he knew that he was predisposed by heredity to mental difficulties. (Mühlher 275–76) The writer's preoccupation with his own potential for mental problems fed, as Ziegler has strongly underscored, on the interest among physicians and authors at that time in madness. This new evaluation of insanity initially arose from the ideas of the Scottish physician John Brown and their influence on German romantics and physicians, including Hoffmann's medical acquaintances in Bamberg, particularly his close friend Dr. Adalbert Marcus. Brown maintained that there were two general diseased conditions, the sthenic state, a condition of over excitement, and the asthenic state, one of nervous weakness. (Ziegler 130) From this basic concept, others quickly drew analogies between body and soul, the inner and the outer world. Such analogies offered a justification for detecting a beneficial quality in insanity, because the asthenic individual became a positive symbol of the romantic movement, a representative of elevated purposes. The night was also, as Ziegler has noted, regarded as asthenic, explaining the imprudence that frequently overcome people at that time of day, while madness was the noble form of this recklessness. (Ziegler 130) A constructive contact with the subconscious through madness is, she concludes, implied in these theories. (Ziegler 130)

A substantial number of physicians were interested in indications of the subconscious, including such scientists as Gotthilf Heinrich Schubert and Johann Christian Reil. Their interests clearly parallel those of several romantic authors, including Hoffmann. Schubert appears to be convinced that the ill person comes nearer a union with his or her inner spirit. In his study *Ansichten von der Nachtseite der Naturwissenschaft*, he states:

Es werden zwar die noch ungeborenen Kräfte eines künftigen daseyns vornehmlich in einem krankhaften oder ohnmächtigen Zustand des jetzigen sichtbar, ...mag auch im gesunden und wachen Zustand der vollkommeneren

Organe, jene dunkle Symphatie entferner Wesen immer wirksamer seyn, sie vermag aber erst in solchen Momenten wie die des magnetischen Schlafs, des Nachtwandelns, Wahnsinns und ähnlichen krankhaften Zuständen hervorzutreten.[7]

Such an outlook on insanity entered Hoffmann's literary production early and was part of the background to the continual depiction of insanity as a state with positive as well as negative features.

The life of the mind is also a primary interest in the frame discussions of the second volume of the collection. Mind control becomes a chief interest in the dialogues of this part of the frame. It is the concept of magnetism that is particularly emphasized by the author. Magnetism is especially seen in the context of its potential for expanding consciousness and perception. As a result, it is hard to be entirely negative to the concept, since it, like insanity, can serve as a leap into the realm of mysterious forces. Magnetism, as part of the outer world of reality, can expose the existence of concealed powers at work in the mind and intensify the inner vision. This ability in magnetism was clearly appealing to the romantics, as it was believed that the subconscious was a foundation for the knowledge of the entire man. The potential of magnetism to open new routes into the inner world captivated Hoffmann, even though at the same time the author feared the loss of control over the individual self, just as he did when encountering insanity.

The substantial degree of medical particulars which the writer introduces in this section is typical of the exceptional fascination also of nonprofessionals in medicine during the romantic period. Hoffmann himself was an ardent reader of medical and quasi-medical works. Magnetism and its potential for good and evil was a primary subject of discussion in the literary circles in which the author participated. Ziegler has observed that although Franz Anton Mesmer's introduction of magnetism was made years before Hoffmann was writing, the intensive work of German physicians kept the concept in the mind of the public. Information about new miracle psychic cures was constantly forthcoming, not only in medical journals, but also in various newspapers. (Ziegler 174–75)

The magnetic state resembled what one would currently refer to as hypnotism, but Mesmer himself did not use the concept. If his patients went into such a state, it was perceived as being coincidental. Mesmer was first and foremost interested in the qualities of the magnet and the magnetic fluid. Magnets, due to their peculiar ability to attract iron, appeared to possess phenomenal powers. Mesmer's work was, as a comprehensive study on the history of psychiatry penned by Franz G. Alexander and Sheldon T. Selesnick underscores, focused on two suppositions: the notion that some individuals were gifted with healing powers; and the classical theories, formulated by the Greeks, that Paracelsus and others revived, that all things stood in a sympathetic mysterious relationship kept together by a fluid.[8] Mesmer attempted to make use of these two common beliefs. He performed as a healer and tried to make his patients believe that they were in contact with the magnetic fluid. They believed they would do whatever their healer told them to do.

Even though suggestible patients may have been hypnotized in such conditions, Mesmer was not interested in this side effect. Instead, he emphasized that through the contact with iron and through hand movements by their healer or "magnetizer" the patients would be "invaded" by the magnetic fluid. This invasion was intended to bring on a crisis with curative powers; when patients woke up, they were expected to feel better.

It is worth noting that Hoffmann does not mention hypnotism, but magnetism. Magnetism and mesmerism, a term introduced by Mesmer's friend Karl Wolfart, were the appellations given to the phenomenon before a Scottish physician, James Braid, later renamed it hypnotism. (Alexander and Selesnick 132)

The exceptional powers erroneously ascribed to the magnetizer during the romantic period were a source of both captivation and worry. During this time, it was commonly believed that the magnetizer could control the subject exclusively by thought. This is a state of affairs which has devastating repercussions in stories like "Der unheimliche Gast" and "Der Magnetiseur." It is the modern point of view that a person under hypnosis cannot be forced to do anything against his will. However, due to the false powers attributed to the hypnotist, the belief was very widespread in the early nineteenth century that only someone who practiced this medicine with a pure heart could cure the patient most effectively and safely.

The high anticipations and deep anxieties which conversations on magnetism frequently lead to dominate the discussions in the Serapion Circle. The first part of their discussion addresses the description of magnetism, as well as different perspectives, favorable as well as unfavorable, on the phenomenon. Their dialogues also have a structural objective as they preface the series of case histories about magnetism that ensue in many of the inner tales.

The direct personal encounters of the *Serapionsbrüder* with magnetism also receive much attention in the frame. Lothar, for instance, is highly skeptical of the phenomenon and cites bad personal experiences as a reason. Another member of the circle, Cyprian, stresses the positive aspects of magnetism. One important argument for Cyprian's enthusiasm is his belief in Mesmer's contention that an ill person in a somnambulistic state is capable of recognizing the symptoms of his malady and discovering what is necessary to cure it.

Another positive feature of magnetism in Cyprian's view is its relationship with music, since magnetism assists us in understanding the psychic principle that deals with the secret harmonies which we otherwise would be incapable of discerning. This comment in the frame anticipates a more detailed conversation in the following inner tale "Die Automate" about the same theme which the author has borrowed directly from Schubert. Mesmer believed in a universal harmony and was himself a gifted musician, frequently presenting his ideas with a musical vocabulary. Since magnetism offers a view into concealed harmonies, it can be of substantial benefit to the artist, who is able to enlarge his consciousness with its assistance.

But strong reservations are also made regarding the advantages of magnetism. Lothar, for instance, fears the phenomenon, not because it is an illusion that hurts people, but rather because he believes that it is authentic and holds the potential for substantial harm. The connection between the mind and the mysterious bond between them emerges here in another context: namely that of the ill but still sane individual subjected to the interfering treatment of the magnetizer and exposed to great potential danger to his mind. One reason for the threat against the sanity of a sick person is the idea of a heightened state of mind. The notion that the ill person was in an exalted state of consciousness frequently appear in medical writings of the period. Lothar turns it around by arguing that expanded consciousness always presupposed an aberration in the relationship between body and soul. This explanation, as Ziegler also notes, leads in several directions for the author, since it connects artistic creativity with sickness and since any exalted state in his characters implies an imbalance, a perilous condition which, if the characters are essentially sound, like Wolfram von Eschenbach in "Der Kampf der Sänger" and Marie in "Nußknacker und Mäusekönig," they can survive. If they, on the other hand, are torn in their inner beings, like Elis Fröbom in "Die Bergwerke zu Falun," they cannot. (Ziegler 181) For that reason, a person in a heightened state of mind is in a perilous position; capable of higher understanding, but not remote from the threat of insanity or annihilation.

The part of the frame which introduces the third volume of *Die Serapionsbrüder* continues the analysis of phenomena such as madness and magnetism. But it also includes comprehensive discussions on other topics, especially views on the role and nature of the Devil and opinions on various supernatural elements (subjects also raised in the introduction to the second volume). The evil one himself appears directly in the story "Nachricht aus dem Leben eines bekannten Mannes." In the discussion of the Serapion Circle the association of insanity with those who make deals with the Devil relates this part of the frame to earlier sections, such as in "Der Kampf der Sänger." The temptation of a pact with Satan, whether for material benefit or supernatural power or knowledge, places a person at risk for both insanity and illegal actions. While Heinrich von der Ofterdingen and Elis Fröbom fell under the spell of evil creatures, neither was guilty of a crime. In the third volume of the collection, several of the tales ("Das Fräulein von Scuderi" is a prime example) address this additional facet of insanity, for which the author's own legal experience and his comprehensive familiarity with medical works provide the foundation.

The members of the circle also touch upon the real nature of supernatural creatures such as ghosts. Their discussions on the subject closely reflect the contents and tendencies of the treatment of the topic in the inner stories. The contributions vary from the serious to the more lighthearted, a variation which is also represented in the inner tales. The less than threatening and slightly ironic depiction of spirits in a story like "Ein Fragment aus dem Leben dreier Freunde," for instance, can be sharply contrasted with the dark and destructive evil present in an account such as "Eine Spukgeschichte."

The frame of the fourth volume deals with totally different and less profound topics, such as a discussion on various disturbers of peace in polite society. The author introduces this subject with the most trivial example of social discourse, a conversation about the weather. The problem of ridding oneself of bores also is addressed by the members of the circle. Such discussions reflect the lightweight content of some of the tales in the last volume, such as "Ästhetische Teegesellschaft." But the topics of conversation eventually become more serious and Cyprian reintroduces the theme of insanity. The emphasis on madness takes the frame full circle by stressing the abnormal mental condition as a dominating theme of the collection.

A story such as "Rat Krespel" combines the theme of insanity with another important Hoffmann theme which has previously been approached in the frame, namely music. It is therefore perhaps natural that this particular tale succeeds the initial frame and the anecdote about Serapion. The unforgettable portrait of Krespel offers a good start for an analysis of the various themes of the often wondrous inner stories of *Die Serapionsbrüder*.

Chapter Four
Madness, Malady and Music:
The Cases of "Rat Krespel" and "Baron von B."

Introduction

It is well-known that music played a very significant part in E. T. A. Hoffmann's life. He was after all a musician, a composer as well as an accomplished conductor. It was therefore natural that the same topic would become a key element also in his literary production. The early narrative "Ritter Gluck" had already initiated a lifelong preoccupation with music. For this writer, music is unquestionably one of the most influential channels through which the demonic, incalculable powers of the universe burst in upon the ordinary, calculable life of man, with an elemental force, and set up tremendous upheavals of the personality. Music therefore also often becomes a topic discussed in direct relation to madness. Numerous stories in the late collection *Die Serapionsbrüder* also reflect that same interest in music as an elemental power. Two of the narratives in the collection, "Rat Krespel" and "Baron von B" (the latter is in fact more of a brief anecdote), are of special importance when one discusses Hoffmann's approach to the fantastic using music as a major tool. Since the story of the extraordinary Krespel immediately succeeds the introductory tale of Serapion it is a logical point of departure for an analysis of the relationship between music, madness and fantastic elements in this collection of tales.

Rat Krespel

The remarkable (and originally untitled) tale of the eccentric Councillor Krespel was first published in *Frauentaschenbuch für das Jahr 1818* in 1818. The narrative became a part of the first volume of *Die Serapionsbrüder* the following year. But the highly creative account had been penned much earlier. The story was in fact completed already in the fall of 1816.

The name of the protagonist and the story of the bizarre way he built his house is based on a real historical character. It was the lawyer and archivist Johann Bernhard Krespel (1747–1813) (portrayed by Goethe in the sixth volume of *Dichtung und Wahrheit* without mentioning him by name) whom Hoffmann had in mind when he wrote the story. Frank Haase has pointed out that another historical person, the Prussian bureaucrat Carl Pistor (1778–1847) provided the author with additional inspiration for the tale. Haase mentions that Pistor was an almost fanatical violinist and opened up violins in order to discover the secret of their sounds; in addition to this, he was a very competent violin maker.[1] From such models from real life, the author has created a distinguished and fascinating character, Councillor Krespel, who clearly is one of his most famous literary figures.

"Rat Krespel" is a tale based on a highly complex narrative technique. Even though the main narrator introduces the action, the events are ultimately depicted from the perspectives of different people. When the initial narrator, Theodor, arrives in H—, the town is in an uproar over the bizarre behavior of a certain Councillor Krespel, whom numerous good citizens consider utterly insane. He is a man of law and a diplomat of eminent distinction and, in return for the services which the Councillor has rendered, a reigning prince has charitably offered to pay for a new house which Krespel has proposed to build. This house is constructed in an extremely unconventional way and without any real building plans. In the finished domicile a magnificent banquet is given by way of a "house-warming," but initially only the workmen are invited. In the evening the wives and daughters arrive, and there is dancing until dawn, with Krespel himself playing the violin and directing the musicians.

The main narrator, Theodor, initially gets acquainted with Krespel at a dinner in the house of professor M—where the Councillor's unconventional conduct as dinner guest excites his interest. The Councillor is actually the uncontested center of attention of many guests. Krespel's surprisingly hostile reaction to a question regarding a young woman, Antonie, increases Theodor's interest, which is even more aroused by information about the remarkable Councillor given by another person present, namely the professor.

It turns out that Krespel had arrived in town several years earlier and had built a house where he supposedly had lived alone with an old housekeeper; everyone in town believing him to be a bachelor. Nevertheless, after he had been absent for a few months, his neighbors saw his home splendidly lighted and then heard music—piano, violin—and a female voice of incredible musical beauty. Later, around midnight that same night, the Councillor's voice is heard in fierce and fervent tones together with another younger masculine voice apparently in reproach, and a woman's sobbing voice. Finally a young man stumbles down the stairs. He gets into a carriage and drives off in despair. The old housekeeper does little to appease the curious neighbors: the Councillor had earlier brought home a beautiful young woman called Antonie. The man arriving later was apparently her fiancé, but Krespel evidently disliked his visit and forced him to leave. To the people in town Antonie remains a mystery. Krespel hardly ever allows her to appear at the window and on the rare occasions when she is with him outside the house, he observes her with "argus eyes." Music is forbidden in her presence, and even though the wonderful voice of that first evening must have been hers, she never sang again, even at home with the Councillor.

The mystery is highly intriguing to Theodor. He dreams of the young woman, and in these dreams he hears Antonie's voice, even singing several of his own compositions, for Theodor, like the author, apart from being a man of the legal profession, is a musician and composer. He suddenly senses a strong urge to become Antonie's angel of rescue and boldly decides to free the young woman from her seemingly cruel confinement. From the professor he has heard of Krespel's unusual hobby of making violins. It is the Councillor's conviction that some secret is concealed in the body of each violin, for he buys rare old instruments at incredible prices, and, after playing them, dissects them to discover the mystery of their tone.

Through his own interest in music, the narrator manages to get closer to the enigmatic Krespel. On Theodor's first visit to the Councillor's home Krespel presents to him his magnificent collection of old and new violins, including an unusual example bearing a wreath of flowers which the owner considers exceptionally valuable.

During his second visit to the house Theodor meets Antonie, who is assisting the Councillor in constructing a violin and he eventually becomes a frequent visitor. One evening Krespel is in a particularly good mood, because he has discovered a definite irregularity, apparently deliberate, in the structure of a Cremona violin. On this occasion, Theodor attempts to entice Antonie to sing, but is prevented from doing so by Krespel who throws him out of the house. The narrator leaves town with a broken spirit.

On a journey several years later Theodor returns to the town. A mysterious, inexpressible sensation of horror possesses him. A burial is taking place in the churchyard. It is Antonie who is taken to her grave. Theodor visits Krespel's house and is firmly convinced that the latter is somehow involved in the young woman's death, especially considering the Councillor's extremely odd behavior.

Confronted by Theodor, Krespel tells the story from his point of view. Traveling in Italy in search of exceptional violins, he meets and marries a famous singer, Angela. Their temperaments are, however, anything but compatible, and when she one day smashes one of his finest violins to pieces he throws her out of the window and leaves her and her homeland. Krespel later finds out that they have a daughter together. When Angela later dies on a trip to Germany the Councillor brings their child, Antonie, to his home. He learns from a physician that music and death are combined in his daughter's very being. As a result of a serious sickness in the chest, continued singing will inevitably kill her. Krespel is thus unwilling to surrender Antonie to her fiancé who is a composer, although the young man loves her for her own sake and has promised never to let her sing a note. The Councillor is perceptively skeptical regarding that pledge. Antonie gives herself up to her father's will and is content with his companionship. In a mysterious way, Krespel's child identifies herself with his most treasured violin, and when her father plays it, she hears her own voice singing. On the night of Antonie's death, Krespel, in what appears to have been a dream, hears her singing, and hears with it the playing of her former fiancé. Having awakened from his sleep, Krespel rushes to Antonie's room, where he finds her lifeless. After having heard Krespel's story, Theodor leaves his home with a new respect for the Councillor in his tragic loneliness.

Even though initially presented in the first person by Theodor, the story "Rat Krespel," as noted, introduces the perspectives of Professor M—, Krespel's housekeeper, Theodor, and, finally, that of Krespel himself. The story has the character of an arabesque. The reader must piece together the different perspectives and draw his own conclusions about what has happened. As a point of departure, from the end rather than from the beginning, the narrator tells the reader about his return to the town of H—at the time when the beautiful Antonie, daughter of Rat Krespel, is being buried. Her father wears a strange homemade coat, a hat draped with crepe strings cocked over one ear, and a black sword belt in which he carries a fiddle bow instead of a weapon. To the narrator, he is slightly similar to thin-skinned insects. He hops on one foot, making strange twists and turns, until he is completely exhausted. His excessive gestures, agile leaps, and peculiar garb are typical of Hoffmann's descriptive technique and suggest to the knowing reader that the writer is presenting him with a strongly ironic caricature.

When Krespel builds his home without using architectural plans, his unpredictable demeanor baffles all the inhabitants of the town as he arbitrarily tells the builders to put windows and doors in the four walls which he has had them erect without openings. After the tragic death of his child, all the violins in his house are draped in black—except for the old master's violin, which is missing. In its place is a cypress wreath, because Krespel has buried the violin with his daughter, since, in some curious ambiguous way, the violin, which Krespel's child had identified with herself, snapped and broke the moment she died.

Professor M—, one of the narrators of the tale, implies that Krespel killed his daughter. The initial narrator, a lawyer, is persuaded of the justification for the accusation against the father for being responsible for Antonie's death. When he visits Krespel after the funeral, he accuses him to his face of murdering her. A malicious ironic smile can be seen on the latter man's face when he proceeds to narrate the occurrences from his point of view. His story initially emphasizes the Italian background to what later occurs. An important confrontation between the spouses comes, as noted, when Krespel's wife, the famous prima donna, in a temperamental eruption breaks his cherished violin and calls him "bestia tedesca!" The incensed Krespel, as mentioned, responds by a highly dramatic defenestration of his spouse. His wife is, however, luckily not harmed. It is only natural that the couple separates after this climactic event and remains so, since Krespel fears that he may actually one day harm her. A few months after this incident, Krespel's wife writes to tell him about the birth of their daughter while at the same time informing him that he has cured her of her egotistical outbursts.

As noted, Antonie comes to live with Krespel almost immediately after her mother's death. Upon learning that she suffers from an incurable malady which is aggravated by her singing, Krespel sternly forbids her to sing. He furthermore drives the young suitor B—from their home, since the latter has encouraged Antonie to sing. Nonetheless, this man apparently manages to get in contact with her one night.

Professor M—is the person who recounts how a young man dashed from Krespel's home one night, after a young woman's voice had been heard singing inside the house. Krespel believes that the young suitor returned the night Antonie died, sang with her, and thereby evidently hastened her death. The happenings around her death are, however, in the usual Hoffmann manner, ambiguous.

In describing the night when his daughter dies, Krespel recounts that he saw B—and Antonie embracing each other while at the same time hearing music but then falling into unconsciousness:

> Krespel sagte, unbegreiflich sei sein Zustand gewesen, in dem er sich befunden, denn eine entsetzliche Angst habe sich gepaart mit nie gefühlter Wonne. Plötzlich umgab ihn eine blendende Klarheit, und in derselben erblickte er B... und Antonien, die sich umschlungen hielten, und sich voll seligem Entzücken anschauten. Die Töne des Liedes und des begleitenden Pianofortes dauerten fort, ohne daß Antonie sichtbar sang oder B... das Fortepiano berührte. Der Rat fiel nun in eine Art dumpfer Ohnmacht, in der das Bild mit den Tönen versank. (*Werke* 5:56)

In Krespel's vision, the music has thus mysteriously taken on a power of its own and no longer even requires performers. When Krespel revives, his state of fear remains and he runs to Antonie's room and finds his daughter dead:

> Als er erwachte, war ihm noch jene fürchterliche Angst aus dem Traume geblieben. Er sprang in Antoniens Zimmer. Sie lag mit geschlossenen Augen, mit holdselig lächelnden Blick, die Hände fromm gefaltet, auf dem Sofa, als schliefe sie und träume von Himmelswonne und Freudigkeit. Sie war aber tot. (*Werke* 5:56)

Since these passages are highly ambiguous, the reader is never precisely certain what happened the night Krespel's child met her death. Due to the curious account of Antonie's death which the Councillor gives the narrator, it is impossible to tell what really happened. Krespel, by his own admission, had bizarre psychological experiences that night. There at least appears to be sufficient proof that Krespel is deranged and therefore by definition an undependable narrator.

Theodor, to whom Krespel told the story of Antonie's death, expressed the belief that the Councillor was in fact insane: "Nicht einen Augenblick zweifelte ich daran, daß Krespel wahnsinnig geworden, der Professor behauptete doch das Gegenteil." (*Werke* 5:47) The inhabitants of the town were led by his odd behavior to consider him out of his mind. Professor M—, on the contrary, maintained that Krespel was quite sane. The reader may believe as he wishes in the matter. Many scholars seem to agree, however, that Krespel, contrary to the superficial appearance, is one of the author's sanest artists. Since he is trapped between the world of the artist and the world of the philistines surrounding him, he takes refuge in eccentric demeanor. Assuming insanity and thereby exhibiting an ambivalent attitude towards art and life, makes Krespel, as Allienne Rimer Becker has also noted, capable of synthesizing his two worlds in a reasonably harmonious fashion. (Becker 158)

In his works, Hoffmann often equated insanity with romantic irony. His "ironic madness" implied a happy escape from what he regarded as philistine narrow-mindedness while replacing such mundane everyday reality with a more profound connection with what he regarded as the true inner life. One critic, Robert Mollenauer, especially underscores the idea that in this author's fiction madness is a form of irony. Mollenauer contends that irony and insanity became for Hoffmann comparable literary substitutes as demonstrated in, for instance, "Rat Krespel." (Mollenauer 224)

Krespel's irony is reflected in his smile. The usual sign to signify the ambivalent ironic view of life in romantic literature is a smile or a laugh behind a mask. In the case in point, the author depicts the expression on Krespel's face as a grotesque mask behind which he laughed with bitter satanic scorn. The text gives the following descriptions emphasizing the almost demonic nature of the protagonist's smile: "...aber bald verzog sich dies Gesicht zur graulichen Maske, aus der recht bitterer, grimmiger, ja wie es mir schien, recht teuflischer Hohn herauslache." (*Werke* 5:36–37) Another example also mentions the diabolic character of the smile: "...diabolisches lächelnde Gesicht ..." (*Werke* 5:42) A third example directly stresses the combination of irony and smiling: "ein boshaftes ironisches Lächeln flog über sein Gesicht." (*Werke* 5:49) Here once again Bellemin-Noël's "rires sardoniques" become part of the picture.

Krespel is one of the writer's most memorable creations. Drawn with a few bald strokes of the pen, the grotesque Councillor, created with deliberate ambiguity and irony, is covered in the veil of the absurd. Krespel is a fine example of the fantastic created by caricature and irony, which the author employs to expose the paradoxes of life. The irony of life hidden beneath the caricature of the fantastic Krespel emerges from the artist's conflict with the philistine world. The preference for the abnormal and bizarre, as exemplified by the character of Krespel, gives Hoffmann's art, as Hermann August Korff, among others, has described it, its characteristic impression. (Korff 599)

The mysterious nature of the main character and his peculiar actions and experiences in "Rat Krespel" is a typical example in Hoffmann's production of what Todorov would consider an "uncanny" narrative. The story begins as an uncanny account and also ends as one. The narrative provides no rational explanation as to the real nature of Antonie's death. It is never made clear if Krespel's bizarre dream actually was just a dream. The reader's hesitation in interpreting this tragic event remains to the very end. It is this essential Todorovian concept of lasting hesitation that motivates the account as "uncanny" rather than "fantastic-uncanny." The latter "borderline" concept would have presupposed some change in the nature of the story in its final part, for instance by offering some kind of natural explanation. But no such change ever appears.

Paradoxically, at least on the surface, "Rat Krespel" may appear to be an essentially realistic tale, despite its very unusual protagonist and the curious events surrounding his person. But even the chosen narrative technique sends a clearly different message to the reader. It is at times a veritable puzzle to ascertain how events actually unfold in the story. The very lack of a natural chronological order of occurrences implies a break with any traditional realistic narrative technique. But what is even more important is the fact that Hoffmann deliberately deceives the reader into concluding things about personalities and events that later turn out to be completely unfounded. The author thus consciously makes rational interpretations based on a straightforward reading extremely unreliable, since they are entirely invalidated by later explanations.

Theodor's somewhat hasty assumption that Krespel is a brutal murderer is a clear case in point. The young narrator reaches such a faulty conclusion because he bases this notion on mistaken assumptions which superficially may seem justified in such bizarre circumstances. But the dependence of the main narrator on rational logic actually leads him completely astray. His statement that reflection leads him to believe that Krespel is a villain thereby becomes a very ironic example of self-deception: "Je mehr ich der Sache nachdachte, desto klarer wurde es mir, daß Krespel ein Bösewicht sein müsse." (*Werke* 5:29) Nothing surrounding the Councillor is quite what it seems. If one were to choose German terms in this context one could thus safely argue that *Schein* sharply contradicts *Sein* in this story.

It should be noted that this search for the real truth is not limited to the more superficial narrative levels of the story. Krespel himself is on a frantic exploration of inner truths and secrets. His strange dissection of his violins in order to discover the real nature of the mystery of the remarkable musical tones his instruments produce could be seen in this context. But as is the case in the main narrator's search for the truth, this probe is essentially futile. Such fruitless attempts to find rational explanations are indeed also a common motif in Hoffmann's literary production. It reappears but to a much lesser degree in the anecdote describing the life of the peculiar figure who goes under the name of "Baron von B."

Baron von B

The short narrative "Baron von B." is one of Hoffmann's lesser known works. It could be argued that, at least in a Todorovian sense, this narrative is only "borderland" fantastic in nature as a closer analysis of the account will also demonstrate. "Baron von B." was written in 1819 and originally published in the *Allgemeine Musikalische Zeitung;* two years later it was integrated in the fourth volume of *Die Serapionsbrüder.*

As is the case with Councillor Krespel, the story of Baron von B. has a real person as a model. Hoffmann had the highly eccentric nobleman Ernst von Bagge in mind when he wrote the anecdote. Von Bagge was a fanatic music lover who also claimed to be an outstanding musician and composer. He had, as did Krespel, a special fascination with the violin. Hoffmann chose to stay very close to what he regarded as von Bagge's real character when he penned his own anecdote.

"Baron von B" relates episodes in the life of a strange nobleman whom some would consider utterly mad and others perhaps simply very eccentric. The succession of bizarre elderly gentlemen, ranging from the satanic to the eccentric, which dominate the tales in the third volume of the collection, ends with the Baron von B., the wealthy violin specialist who plays the instrument in a strongly revolting manner. The preceding five accounts all included satanic figures or individuals possessed by demonic powers, at times to the point of insanity. Baron von B., like them, is also possessed and definitely somewhat crazy, but he is far from evil. His evident knowledge of violin technique appears disproportionate in relation to his accurate ear for defects in the assiduous playing of his pupils.

The baron's peculiar personality brings to mind two previously presented figures, Serapion and Rat Krespel. As does Serapion, the baron has a twisted perception of reality; and like him, he is an *artist manqué* because of this failure. Like Krespel, Baron von B. has an intense love affair with the violin, but Krespel cannot give himself fully to the inner mystery of music; he constantly attempts to tear apart violins to find out what actually produces their tone.

The baron is extremely eager to share what he considers to be his great talent and also has supposedly admiring pupils in order to be able to boast about his unsurpassed mastery of his beloved instrument. On several occasions, he even pays young men to become his pupils. The baron thereby conveniently creates a mentor-student relationship which, at least on the surface, enables him to have virtually total control over these young and impressionable men.

The baron's obsession with violins becomes particularly interesting if the instrument is regarded as a symbol of something else. James McGlathery, among others, has pointed out that the violin has a shape not unlike the female figure, only in miniature. McGlathery concludes that the baron may well have the love of women in mind when he talks about mastering the violin.[2]

Such a symbolic interpretation of the role of the instrument also lends further support to the notion that this story should not be considered simply as a straightforward humorous anecdote, even though humor is a very strong element almost constantly present in the tale. It is important to note that the baron is very capable of hearing flaws in the musical efforts of his pupils even though he himself is anything but a first-rate musician. At times, his ability to actually perceive what could be considered the perfect ideal of music despite his own obvious limitations as a musical performer seems to be almost uncanny. It is the musical excellence of Tartini which is his ideal and (almost like an imperfect revenant of the famous composer) the baron appears to have Tartini's ear but not his active musical ability. At least in this limited sense, one could argue that the baron is possessed by demonic powers that are not rationally explicable. This is also what makes this story at least "borderline" uncanny in the Todorovian sense (as for its companion piece "Rat Krespel"). Since no real attempt is made to logically explain this specific musical ability, the story remains, in spite of its clearly humorous nature, uncanny to the very end and the tale thus provides an interesting example of an important subcategory (the "uncanny") in Todorov's model for an analysis of the fantastic genre.

The portrayal of the humorous baron, as Vickie Ziegler has also previously underscored, foreshadows the circle discussion of the playwright Zacharias Werner. (Ziegler 248) Like the Baron, Werner does not have a firm grip on reality. The author even alleges that Werner took the vision of another existence for real life in his madness. (*Werke* 5:219) The baron, in the belief that he and one other old man are the exclusive heirs to the skills of the great Tartini, lives in a dream that he takes for reality. Despite his eccentricity, the baron seems to be a genuine artist. Hoffmann portrays him in phrases reminiscent of his depictions of other artists in *Die Serapionsbrüder*. The baron's particular insanity is not, as Ziegler also notes, intended to obscure his authentic value for music, just as Werner's derangement never prevented him from producing literary works. (Ziegler 248)

The circle member relating the story, Cyprian, supports his narration on information offered to him by a renowned virtuoso, but he recounts the tale as if he himself were that musician. This technique contrasts drastically with the one used for Theodor's lengthy account about his confrontation with gambling. In that anecdote, Theodor described his own encounter with the perilous temptation of the dice, thereby providing a persuasive immediacy which further stressed the central point of the short tale "Spielerglück." In the case of the story about Baron von B., Cyprian gives an elegant form to a brief account presented to him. Cyprian's method of narration makes the anecdote he tells more remote from firsthand experience than Theodor's. Cyprian's story is, however, less detached from reality than an inner tale with its own proper appellation.

The rather simple narrative perspective from which the life of Baron von B. is told contrasts sharply with the exceedingly complicated narrative structure of "Rat Krespel." But the two stories nonetheless have much in common. Music is of course the element that truly binds them together. But another theme is almost as important: the role of the main character as a person with what appears to be demonic powers, be those powers in the form of a virtually hypnotic control over another human being or in the form of a supernatural musical ear. These qualities indeed make the Councillor and the baron demonic, even though none of them could be considered evil. A combination of demonic power *and* evil is, however, otherwise typical of several of Hoffmann's literary creations. His stories abound with devilish characters and at least on one occasion the Devil himself becomes the protagonist, though in a somewhat more benevolent disguise. The "real" Devil and "minor" devils who in one way or another faithfully imitate the supreme Prince of Darkness is a major Hoffmann theme of the fantastic that merits a closer look with the real Devil himself as a rather obvious point of departure.

Chapter Five

Devils and Vampires: "Nachricht aus dem Leben eines Bekannten Mannes," "Der unheimliche Gast," "Die Brautwahl" and "Vampirismus"

Introduction

It has often been pointed out that Hoffmann's production is full of demonic characters, at times directly comparable to the devil himself. Such demons also exemplify one of the most important themes in Todorov's (and Vax's) list of fantastic elements. It is true that Hoffmann's diabolical figures frequently represent inner demons that torment the characters of a story. What a scholar like Hans Toggenburger has referred to as "Der Dämon Eigenliebe" plays a significant role in this regard. According to this idea, man considers his personal qualities and abilities as admirable, but is at the same time incapable of understanding that they are an expression of his inner world of perception. He therefore often uses his abilities for questionable purposes such as control of his fellow men through means such as magnetism.[1]

But apart from such inner demons, Hoffmann's tales can also include figures whose evil appears to exist totally outside the characters of normal human beings, an evil that can stand quite well on its own. It is in this light a highly fantastic story like "Nachricht aus dem Leben eines bekannten Mannes" can be best understood.

Nachricht aus dem Leben eines Bekannten Mannes

"Nachricht aus dem Leben eines bekannten Mannes," (also at times referred to as "Der Teufel in Berlin"), was written in early 1819 and published in the magazine *Der Freimüthige* in the same year, which was, as Otto Pniower points out the same magazine in which Hoffmann had seen his first work in print sixteen years earlier. The account was later included in the third volume of *Die Serapionsbrüder*.

"Nachricht aus dem Leben eines bekannten Mannes" is loosely based on Peter Hafftitz' comprehensive chronicle *Microchronicon Marchicum* (written in 1595) and takes place in the mid-sixteenth century shortly after the death of Martin Luther and begins when a mysterious stranger, remarkably well-dressed and of dignified demeanor, surfaces suddenly in the Brandenburgian capital and through his winsome deportment and his exceptional gallantries, makes himself well-liked in society despite some very curious habits: he is somewhat lame, but if someone extends a helping hand, he may well leap several meters in the air with his helper and descend twelve paces away:

> Reichte ihm nun einer die Hand, so sprang er mit ihm wohl an die sechs Ellen hoch in die Luft, und kam über die Gosse hinweg zwölf Schritte davon auf die Erde nieder. Das verwunderte die Leute ein wenig und mancher verstauchte sich hin und wieder auch wohl das Bein. (*Werke* 7:8)

This is of course an obviously fantastic occurrence. The fantastic element is mitigated through the use of irony. The citizens of Berlin are "verwundert" to be sure, but the explanation they receive is quite peculiar:

> Der Fremde entschuldigte sich damit, daß er sonst, als noch sein Fuß nicht lahm, an dem Hofe des König von Ungarn Vortänzer gewesen, daß ihm daher, verhelfe man ihm nur zu einigem Springen, gleich die alte arge Lust anwandle, und daß er wider seinen Willen dann erschrecklich in die Luft fahren müsse, als tanze er noch zur selbiger Zeit. (*Werke* 7:8)

The people of the city are calmed by this explanation focusing on the stranger's background as a dancer. The rational reader detects the author's irony; and the whole scene is even treated as amusing fiction.

But the stranger's bizarre behavior does not stop there. At night he knocks at the doors of his friends, dressed in white grave clothes and the following day explains himself by stating that he only wanted to remind his fellow men of the temporary nature of life. Even the Elector of Brandenburg becomes interested in the stranger and offers him a position in the government. The form taken by this "well-known" man is thus anything but sinister. He is a good-natured and highly appreciated burgher who on the surface possesses all the conventional middle-class virtues. Apart from this general depiction of his character and the surrounding events, the single anecdote that makes up the account addresses the relations of this stranger with an old midwife (and witch) named Barbara Roloffen, an old women servant who has caused her employer's spouse to bear a hideous ogre instead of a normal baby. Satan is forced to demonstrate the power of his real identity in order to rescue this female representative of evil. He disappears in the form of a giant black bat after saving the old woman from being burned as a witch. The choice of the bat as an object of the supernatural transformation is a direct illustration of the key defining element in the fantastic genre which Louis Vax has referred to as "histoire de vampire." (*Séduction...*, 308) Andrzej Zgorzelski's description of fantastic motifs such as bats, vampires and ghosts as "a stimulation of the reader's feeling of wonder and marvel when facing the unknown" also fits well into this context. (Zgorzelski 299)

Despite the horrifying ending, this tale is essentially humorous in nature. The narrating persona is (by means of irony) the reason that the rational reader need not to be too concerned regarding what he is reading about the activities of the Prince of Darkness. An alternative way of presenting the story could have been to omit all ironic elements; but in this case the rational reader would have been confronted with a strong assault on his standards of everyday causality.

The Serapion Circle responds to this anecdote in various ways, ranging from ironic smiles to profound earnestness. Even though Theodor suffers greatly from an illness, he remains in a much more optimistic frame of mind than his friend Lothar. Theodor's good spirits assist him in defeating his malady whereas Lothar despondently spends his time reading accounts about Satan in ancient chronicles. The latter's fixation on earlier history may have more importance than a cursory motivation for the presentation of the story "Nachricht aus dem Leben eines bekannten Mannes." His fascination with the topic could also be due to his slightly dangerous frame of mind. On occasions when the established order of life appears threatened for the author's characters, as Robert Mühlher has stressed, the demons become stronger. Mühlher also observes that the more corrupt or desperate a person is, the less able he is to discern whether it is an angel or a demon who confronts him. (Mühlher 436–39) Lothar's depressed disposition makes him hate existence and he explains that when his depression was severe, the Devil appeared to him during sleepless nights. (Werke 7:14) The same combination of anxiety and irony found in the narrative is also evident, as Hans Joachim Kruse has noted, in Lothar's comment that he feels terror at the Devil's presence and nonetheless is prepared to employ him as an aide in his penmanship.[2]

In order to restore the more lighthearted tone surrounding the anecdote and relieve the darkness of evil which is unquestionably also present, Hoffmann lets the members of the circle carry on a not too somber debate regarding the most successful type of satanic figure. The Serapion members conclude that German devils are preferable to imported Italian ones, such as Trabacchio, Dapertutto and Coppola. The native variety, even though he is still an evil force, is at least "gemütlich," meticulous and punctual. He does, it cannot be denied, allow himself to be outwitted, and he has a disagreeably mocking side, but that does not matter much. Moreover, opposition is expressed here to furnishing the devil with any traits that go to extremes, such as those found in literary works of the time: "Entweder wird der Teufel zum gemeinen Hanswurst, oder das Grauenhafte, Unheimliche zerreist das Gemüt". (Werke 7:20)

One of the members of the circle, Lothar, summarizes the author's suggested new type of literary devil: " ...genug, die Sache bleibt für uns rein phantastisch, und selbst das unheimliche Spukhafte, das sonst dem 'furchtbar verneinenden Prinzip der Schöpfung' beiwohnt, kann, durch den komischen Kontrast, indem es erscheint, nur jenes seltsame Gefühl hervorbringen, das, eine eigentümliche Mischung des Grauenhaften und Ironischen, uns auf gar nicht unangenehme Weise spannt." (Werke 7:15) But with this statement, the demonic nature of the tale does not disappear completely, because Lothar goes on to state that the dread of the account of the witch has affected him profoundly. (Werke 7:16)

The somewhat less somber atmosphere in "Nachricht aus dem Leben eines bekannten Mannes" and in a comparable tale like "Die Brautwahl" separates it from some of the dark seriousness which often colors Hoffmann's approach to these themes, particularly in later sections of the third volume of the collection. The remoteness in time from the author's own era is important: Satan is here safely relegated to a period when people still believed in him—at least a possible implication that Hoffmann does not. The mixture of horrifying and ironic elements in the story stimulates the reader, as Lothar notes just after the end of the story, stressing the function of ghost stories as tales that, with their combination of terrifying and comical features affects the reader in a not altogether "unpleasant way." (*Werke* 7:15)

This response, caused by encounters with the supernatural, has, as has also been observed by Vickie Ziegler, similarities with the "pleasant shivering" to which Dagobert refers at the beginning of the narrative "Der unheimliche Gast." (Ziegler 222)

In the story of the Devil as a strange visitor in Berlin, as well as in accounts such as "Die Brautwahl" and "Der Kampf der Sänger," either the period depicted or the choice of characters from a faraway past has a distancing effect on the perceived menace of demonic power. The exact date of the allusion to the Hafftitz chronicle at the beginning of the tale is intended to lend credibility to the occurrences described, be it with a somewhat ironic smile in this case.

The initial part of "Nachricht aus dem Leben eines bekannten Mannes" appears to have a somewhat calming impact on the reader since he at that point regards the Devil as an essentially benign elderly gentleman and a largely normal Berlin resident, who attends weddings, offers gifts, and participates in dancing despite his lame foot. Karl Olbrich observes in his essay "E.T.A. Hoffmann und der deutsche Volksglaube" that the author often embodies this evil principle in a human figure, who appears suddenly in the family circle. Such an unexpected appearance is characteristic of the Devil in this story as well as of Count S in "Der unheimliche Gast."[3]

In sharp contrast to the innocent beginning of the story, the second part of the narrative makes the Devil the dominating figure and at this point he demonstrates his real personality. Barbara Roloffin's behavior when she sees the stranger at the Lütkens house is, as Ziegler has noted, remarkably comparable to that of Marguerite, Angelika's French companion in "Der unheimliche Gast." (Ziegler 222) In both cases, a noticeable change is evident in their appearance and conduct. Marguerite, as is Barbara, is under the influence of evil powers. (Ziegler 222) The full extent of the relationship between the Devil and the old midwife becomes apparent only in the final part of the narrative. At that time, she has confessed to being a witch and has been helped by the stranger who, as mentioned, chooses to turn himself into a bat, and thereby gives the story an additional vampire-like quality. This horrifying display is especially effective considering the benevolent nature of the stranger early in the account. In its approach to supernatural occurrences, the story points ahead to a tale like "Erscheinungen." The Devil-like characters have clear similarities to figures appearing in accounts such as "Die Brautwahl," "Der unheimliche Gast," "Fräulein von Scuderi" and "Eine Vampyrgeschichte."

The function of the Devil as a personified representative of evil in Hoffmann's oeuvre should also be seen in the context of the author's general concept of good and evil. The polarity of these positive and negative forces is to be understood in terms of the philosophy of Friedrich Schelling, since, as Karl Ochsner has outlined, the author's concept of good and evil is essentially the same as that formulated by Schelling in the philosopher's work *Philosophische Untersuchungen über das Wesen der Menschlichen Freiheit* (1809), from which Ochsner quotes the following important ideas:

> Alles Leben aber geht nur durch das Feuer des Widerspruches. Ohne Widerspruch wäre keine Bewegung, kein Leben, kein Fortschritt, sondern ewiger Stillstand, ein Todesschlummer aller Kräfte. Das Böse ist zur Offenbarung der Liebe Gottes nötig. 'Denn Jedes Wesen kann nur in seinem Gegenteil offenbar werden. Liebe nur in Haß, Einheit nur in Streit.'[4]

Life must thus pass through the fire of contradiction in order to exist and progress. Evil makes man long for the good. Good comes from evil, and, in Ochsner's words, "Das Böse ist also die Bedingung des Guten." (Ochsner 117)

In many of Hoffmann's characters, this struggle between positive and negative powers dominates their life. But when the Devil himself is deeply involved, which he most definitely is in *Nachricht aus dem Leben eines bekannten Mannes,* the good which exists on the surface (the Devil as a nice old gentleman) is purely imaginary, and only the pure evil is real, something which the end of the story illustrates in a colorful way.

"Nachricht aus dem Leben eines bekannten Mannes" is by and large a humorously fantastic tale. Approaching the nature of the fantastic in this anecdote from Todorov's analytical viewpoint, makes one conclusion unavoidable: it is not only the humor that separates the story from many of Hoffmann's accounts of demonic figures. The different nature of the fantastic is even more important. The hesitation of the reader which is a logical result of the action until near the end of the narrative, is replaced by complete disbelief when the devil changes himself into a vampire. This surprising turnaround places the tale in Todorov's category of "the fantastic-marvelous." Many of the author's works emphasize a natural explanation as the ultimate solution to an uncanny mystery (thereby placing them in Todorov's category of the "fantastic-uncanny." In "Nachricht aus dem Leben eines bekannten Mannes," however, the opposite solution is chosen.

The humor which is present in the remarkable tale of the devil's adventures in Berlin is not as prevalent in another story with a demonic main character, "Der unheimliche Gast." In the latter, the darkness of evil comes into the picture much earlier in the story. It is a narrative worth reading also as a contrast to the much less somber "Nachricht aus dem Leben eines bekannten Mannes."

Der unheimliche Gast

"Der unheimliche Gast" was written in 1818 and initially published in *Der Erzähler* the following year. In 1820, this complex narrative became part of *Die Serapionsbrüder*.

The tale begins with a scene in which old friends and acquaintances gather round a fire on a stormy night in the late fall when nature shows its most menacing side and discuss mysterious threats which lie just beyond the reach of the hearth and the comfortable rooms. In this sense, the story forms a direct parallel to the frame of the collection. This "mini-frame" structure of an inner story within the larger collection and its larger frame could at least indirectly be considered an example of Bellemin-Noël's definition of a fantastic narrative as a story with a second tale in reduced proportions embedded in it.

"Der unheimliche Gast" is an account which has the middle-aged and enigmatic Italian count as its key figure. Count S is a renowned expert in mysterious arts, possessed of inexplicable powers which could be considered mesmeric or at least covered by the indefinite extension of the mesmeric principle even though Hoffmann prefers to talk about "magnetism." The count decides to use his magnetic power on a young woman with the purpose of conquering her when he sees a miniature picture of her. It is worth noting that this is not the only time that Hoffmann makes such use of pictures. In his essay "E.T.A. Hoffmann und der deutsche Volksglaube," Karl Olbrich ties the author's use of pictures in this tale to the widespread notion that there was a direct link between a picture and the person it portrays. (Olbrich 68–69) It should perhaps be mentioned that examples of another old popular belief can also be found in "Der unheimliche Gast," namely the expectation that the Devil (in this case personified by the evil Count S) tends to suddenly appear whenever his name is mentioned by someone.

The devilish count's schemes in regard to the woman whose picture he has seen (she is named Angelika) quickly takes a serious turn when his powers affect her health. Angelika lies severely ill from the shock at the report of the death of a young officer named Moritz to whom she is engaged to be married. Marguerite, her French governess, and secretly the count's accomplice, continually whispers his name in her ears and sometimes the count himself emerges and scrutinizes the sleeping girl for a long time. For a time, Angelika tries to keep her distance in relation to the count. The key to her feelings about him lies in her identification of him with the devil-figure in a dream that she has had on the night of her fourteenth birthday. But she eventually succumbs to his spell and agrees to marry him. On her wedding day she falls into a strange swoon which the visiting physician refers to as a "magnetic condition." Angelika in fact has come under the control of the count even before she meets him through the medium of her dreams.

The invidious count is also able to exercise his powers from a distance and receive communication through telepathy. One time in Naples he had gained magnetic influence over the fiancée of a Russian officer, Boleslav, and taken her from him, and thereafter killed her through mysterious remote control. The count continually pursues his former competitor with nocturnal horrors in which he himself appears or in which doors accompanied by loud frightening noises open and shut themselves, events which seem ghostly at the time being, since the Russian assumes that he has killed his clandestine rival in a duel. Some of the count's activities, however, are clearly infernal, but nonetheless, altogether human schemes, which include the marriage with Angelika.

The tale has been given a happy ending by the author. In a dream, Angelika sees Moritz, earlier reported dead, returning to her safe and sound. She regards this young man as the guardian angel who has saved her from a satanic seducer. The count suddenly dies the very day he is to be married to Angelika. Many questions regarding why these things happen are deliberately left unanswered by the author.

In addition to the parallelism of the subplots, the author fills the tale with constantly reappearing motifs, such as dreams, pictures, and curious sounds. The sound motif, which initiates the tale by mentioning the whistling of a tea kettle and the storms of the fall season, elements which both complement a vivid discussion of ghosts among some of the characters, eventually proceeds to bizarre noises in nature, including the devil's voice ("Teufelstimme") of Ceylon, an often recurring motif in this collection of narratives, and the terrible groans which torment Bogislav. In a long passage, Moritz's friend Dagobert proposes that the reason such sounds in nature unsettle us is because the forces of nature wish to punish us for our falling away from the universal harmony that reigned in the Golden Age: "...vielleicht liegt darin die Strafe der Mutter, deren Pflege, deren Zucht wir entartete Kinder entflohen." (*Werke* 7:105) At the time of the original harmony no such terror or dread troubled us, whereas now sounds of nature may fill us with fear:

> Ich meine, daß in jener goldnen Zeit, als unser Geschlecht noch im innigsten Einklange mit der ganzen Natur lebte, kein Grauen, kein Entsetzen uns verstörte, eben weil es in dem tiefsten Frieden, in der seligsten Harmonie alles Seins keinen Feind gab, der dergleichen über uns bringen konnte. (*Werke* 7:105–06)

Dagobert is not the only person hinting at the furious forces of nature, which castigate those who attempt to make use of her secrets for their own nefarious purposes. Count S alerts us to the same danger. The association of Dagobert's comments with the insights of the count is that the magnetizer, who in a sense attempts to get himself in touch with the concealed secrets of nature, comes into conflict with these powers, since his objective is not so much to reconnect with original harmonies but instead to utilize these forces for his personal gain. The count for that reason becomes the enemy.

As the emergence of sounds which provoke terror within the characters escalate—starting with sounds of the tea kettle and the autumnal storms, and proceeding to Ceylonese "Luftmusik" the atmospheric noise in Spain, and the horrifying noises of specters at an inn—the discussion approaches the limits of conscious knowledge of concealed powers. At this point, Angelika refers to her peculiar dreams which paralyze her with fright. These dreams are like the one on her fourteenth birthday, which petrified her for several days. As the reader later learns, this dream was the result of the count's first bid to set himself in magnetic contact with the young girl.

A repetition of the very beginning of the story occurs at the end, where Angelika, Moritz and the family sit around the fire on a cold autumn evening, much like the one on which Count S appeared, and annoying noises are themselves heard. Now, the sounds of nature seem harmonious rather than menacing as they originally did. The final pleasant environment is reminiscent of the Golden Age which Dagobert enthusiastically depicts at the beginning of the tale. Now when danger from forces that have disturbed the harmony of nature is past, the beautiful voices of nature appear as agreeable as they must have done in ancient times.

In an essay on the approach to the fantastic as a structural model in Hoffmann's work, Monika Schmitz-Emans has pointed out the many direct parallels between "Der unheimliche Gast" and a story from the earlier collection, *Fantasiestücke,* entitled "Der Magnetiseur." She particularly stresses the remarkable similarity between the two protagonists Count S and the physician Alban, characters that represent exactly the same type of individual. It is also important to note that the relationship between the frame and the actual story is dealt with in a very similar fashion in both narratives. The conclusions of the two stories, however, vary greatly. In "Der unheimliche Gast," the female main character happily rushes out into the arms of her fiancé after having been liberated from the evil spells of the count. In "Der Magnetiseur," the corresponding woman protagonist, on the other hand, dies as a result of the evil manipulations of the magnetizer.

"Der unheimliche Gast" is a superb case in point when Hoffmann is scrutinized with the basis of the analytical framework of Todorovian principles of the pure fantastic. The reader remains baffled by the powers that have been demonstrated by the count and these forces are never really explained at the end of the story. We only learn that they are not unlimited (as proven by the death of the count and his failure to ultimately destroy Angelika). The female protagonist's dream is the only case where the Count is directly and unquestionably compared to the devil himself. But his general demeanor and the demonic nature of his actions, nevertheless, clearly identify his as a diabolical character. In Todorov's theoretical system, Count S exemplifies a creature based on the idea of a "theme of the other" even though he is definitely not a supernatural being per se. His supernatural talents, however, are used to assist in gaining results with regards to a classic theme of the other, namely sexual desire. Such elements can also be found in another account where a devilish figure makes his mark: "Die Brautwahl."

Die Brautwahl

"Die Brautwahl" was written in the spring of 1819 and published in the third volume of the collection one year later after having appeared previously in the *Berlinischer Taschenkalender* (in the same year as it was produced).

The setting for this story is also Berlin. Edmund Lehsen is a talented young artist living in the capital. His maladroit behavior when he first meets the beautiful Albertine Voßwinkel at an art exhibition has clear similarities with the calamities of the bumbling student Anselmus in "Der goldne Topf." The young artist bends down to pick up Albertine's handkerchief, the two heads crash together, he starts back, and at the first step treads on the pug dog of an old lady and at the second on the gouty foot of a professor. Aroused by the commotion, people rush from the neighboring rooms and scold Edmund. The would-be artist also is frequently temporizing with his artistic equipment, which he seems unable to carry without incident. The young man yearns for Italy, the homeland of art, but nevertheless chooses not to go there. Edmund falls in love (or at least thinks he does) with the attractive face of Albertine, who is a somewhat different version of Veronica. Leonhard the goldsmith has known the young artist from his early childhood and designs a plan to defeat Edmund's two rivals for Albertine's hand. The rivals are the Geheimer Kanzlei-Sekretär Tusman, a former schoolmate of Albertine's father, described as bald and ugly, and Baron Dümmerl. The latter suitor fills the Kommisionsrat Voßwinkel with horror by demonstrating that his pocketbook would be seriously imperiled if he were to refuse his daughter's hand to either of these suitors. This competition for the young woman sets the stage for the humorous continuation of the story.

There are two typical Hoffmanesque background tales included in the account: one relates to Manasse, a Jew, the other to the goldsmith, Leonhard. Manasse is in fact, it later turns out, the "Münzjude" Lippold who was actually already executed in 1572 for being involved in black magic, and now wanders around the world, as a second Ahaverus, the traditional "wandering Jew." Leonhard is also strongly suspected of being a ghost, and was known in his previous life as Leonhard Turnhäuser. In the commentary to his edition of *Die Serapionsbrüder*, Hans Joachim Kruse points out that Hoffmann portrays the Swiss goldsmith in a very different light compared to the chronicler Hafftitz, who presented him as a charlatan. Master Leonhard was a chemist, alchemist, physician, astrologer and collector of plants and minerals. As the personal physician of the Elector of Brandenburg in the late sixteenth century, he quickly became famous among the kings and queens of Europe. (Kruse 611)

Hoffmann decides to approach this character in a less traditional way than was done before. Here he uses his earlier portrayal of Francesco in the novel *Die Elixiere des Teufels* for some eerie distraction. The wandering Jew character, the revenant figure, the artist type and other such motifs also appear to be in large part derived from that narrative. A touch of demonry is then added to Leonhard by making him a goldsmith (as is Cardillac in "Das Fräulein von Scuderi"). Edmund and Albertine could be said to correspond to Olivier and Madelon in the same story. A comical *Spießbürger*, Tusmann, completes the picture. A generally rather thin plot is thereby established and presented with only slight variation.

Two components in the narrative are particularly interesting. One is the Jewish "Dales" legend, which, although having little direct bearing on the main story line, is fascinating in itself. Dales is an allegorical character standing for poverty, a figure who enters a household and becomes even larger and more robust as the poverty of the family worsens. This absorbing character was not, unfortunately, utilized or varied in any other story by the author. The other interesting component is included in the conversation between Leonhard and Edmund regarding a piece of art called "eine schöne Baumgruppe nach der Natur" on which Edmund is working. Leonhard remarks about this painting:

> ... Ich meine, aus den dicken Blättern da guckten allerlei Gestalten heraus im buntesten Wechsel, bald Genien, bald seltsame Tiere, bald Jungfrauen, bald Blumen. Und doch sollte das Ganze wohl nur sich zu jener Baumgruppe uns gegenüber gestalten durch die die Strahlen der Abendsonne so lieblich funkeln. (Werke 7:37–38)

This is one of the author's more convincing portrayals of landscape mythology, examples of which also abound in tales like "Das fremde Kind" and "Die Königsbraut." But this mythical landscape otherwise only occasionally appears in the story itself which is dominated by the atmosphere of the real world where a clash between good and evil is presented.

The confrontation between positive and negative powers in "Die Brautwahl," as opposed to the situation in some other Hoffmann tales such as the fairytale world of the *Märchen* "Nußknacker and Mausekönig" and "Das fremde Kind," takes place in the real world of the Prussian capital. The *Münzjude* Lippold, a clearly demonic character, clashes with Meister Leonhard, who appears capable of defeating him. The primary distinction between these revenants and figures from the world of spirits, such as Tinte-Pepser in "Das fremde Kind," is that the revenants are historical characters rather than creatures of fantasy. The connection between their recorded demise and their reappearance in the present is never conclusively explained.

The baffled amazement and disbelief which these two figures cause among the other characters in the story can be exemplified by the reaction to Leopold's exceptionally vivid portrayal of life in the sixteenth century. A surprised Tusmann remarks in response to Leonhard's colorful depictions of an era which is long gone:

> "Mein verehrtester Herr Professor" rief er endlich im Falsett, den ihm die höchste Freude abzunötigen pflegte, "mein teuerster, verehrtester Herr Professor, was sind das für herrliche Dinge, von denen Sie so lebhaft zu erzählen belieben, als wären Sie selbst dabei gewesen?" (*Werke* 7:33)

The use of the subjunctive form "wären" here underscores the incredulity, but later in the story few such skeptical reservations are made when Leonhard demonstrates his extraordinary abilities. He also immediately rejects any notion that he would be untruthful when he claims to have lived in the sixteenth century. (Werke 7:33)

Meister Leonhard, who is consistently in control of the occurrences in the narrative, instantly offers some clues regarding whose side he is on in the battle of wills. Even though his eyes flash, frequently a sign of evil in the author's production, his forehead is free and open, parts of his attire date from the sixteenth century (which previous tales in the collection, such as "Meister Martin der Küfner und seine Gesellen," have portrayed as an era in which art and artisan were in harmony) and he announces that he is an artist. Throughout the account, the reader is never totally sure what to expect from this figure, since the scope of his abilities is never completely transparent. It is also hard to know who he actually is, something which he himself readily acknowledges: "Ei, mein liebes Kind, begann der Goldsmied lächelnd, sehr schwer wird es mir zu sagen, wer ich eigentlich bin. Mir geht es so wie vielen, die weit besser wissen, wofür sie die Leute halten, als was sie eigentlich sind." (Werke 7:91)

This unknown aspect of his character assists in increasing the narrative tension; whether Master Leonhard is relating vivid and detailed accounts about the Berlin of the sixteenth century, outfoxing the notorious *Münzjude* Lippold or removing the green from Tusmann's face, he is confronting Edmund, Tusmann, Albertine and the privy councillor with spheres whose existence they only barely perceive or of which they are completely unaware. Leonhard wants what is good for the characters on whose lives he has an impact; Leonhard even assists these figures in reaching objectives which he himself might consider less than perfect, as for instance Edmund's suggested engagement to Albertine. His ambition is not personal benefit or prosperity, but the promotion of art.

In sharp contrast to Leonhard, who was in the sixteenth century a talented goldsmith so respected at the court in the capital that he had caused great envy among his competitors, Lippold has become an ally of evil powers with the purpose of acquiring money and control. All his endeavors in sorcery are intended to gain gold and authority and continue in that vein.

The revenants raise, in an especially arresting fashion, the issue regarding what is still with us from the past, since the revenant is an historical figure whom the poet, who sees with an inner eye, is able to reinterpret. He belongs in his period, but nonetheless wears some much more recent attire exactly as Leonhard does. Not only his clothes but also his memory, distinguish him as an intermediary character. What for other people is history is for Leonhard individual reminiscence. As a result of this, he is able to discuss Edmund's childhood in pretty much the way that he talks about the history of the city hall tower. A character such as this artist shows some of the unexpected potential in human life because he is firmly based in history as well as in the present. This is indeed one of the major themes of *Die Serapionsbrüder*. This is why the narrator emphasizes the historical illusions connected with such figures, as well as the timeless aspect of such a character—as in this case Leonhard's association with Edmund's early childhood. The unfamiliar dimensions of human existence which the reader senses are present in Leonhard forebode the unusual powers which Count S and Cardillac (another goldsmith) possess in two other tales from the this short story collection. It could be said that Lippold has essentially the same type of personality as these two individuals, whereas Leonhard stands in direct contrast to them. Neither his artistic talent nor his affinity with higher forces has ruined his inner spirit.

In order to reach their objectives, both the revenants in "Die Brautwahl" possess substantial supernatural powers, something which, as Margot Kuttner has also noted in her Hoffmann study, is rather typical of the author's mixing of fairy tale elements with prosaic features. (Kuttner 66) No character in the story is totally unaffected by these forces; Tusmann, the stereotypical Prussian bureaucrat, is the main victim, even though his old friend Voßwinkel has frightening moments as well. If the fantastic can impact even such rigidly controlled existences as theirs, then can influence anyone. While a character such as Tusmann might never be sufficiently weaned from his pedantry to wander in the realm of fantasy, whereas Edmund can be. The author, speaking through Theodor, motivates the encroachment of fantasy upon reality, because it is the most extraordinary aspect of life since it is accessible to anyone if it is firmly grounded in everyday existence: "Ich meine, daß die Basis der Himmelsreiter, auf der man hinaufsteigen will in höhere Regionen, befestigt sein müsse im Leben, so daß jeder nachzusteigen vermag." (*Werke* 7:101–102) Since individuals of Tusmann's and Voßwinkel's type lack a sufficient amount of imagination, they rarely climb this ladder into the realm of the fantastic without the application of external coercion, such as that being used by the master artist in "Die Brautwahl."

This foundation in life, in everyday existence, which is apparent in the historical references in the biographies of the revenants, appears in the other figures as well, all of whom have some discernible association with the Prussian capital. In this sense, this tale has more in common with a story such as "Nußknacker and Mausekönig" (where the Stahlbaums seem to be part of the everyday world) than it does with the symbolic figures in the *Märchen* "Das fremde Kind." The abundance of everyday elements which characters like Leonhard and Lippold come into contact with, play a definite part in Lothar's comment following the story concerning the inclusion of fairy tale elements in a contemporary story: "Übrigens gewahrt ihr, daß ich meinem Hange, das Märchenhafte in der Gegenwart, in das wirkliche Leben zu versetzen, wiederum treulich gefolgt bin." (*Werke* 7:101) Several of the figures that encounter the fantastic in everyday existence have counterparts in other accounts included in the collection. Examples are Edmund who has similarities with Traugott in "Der Artushof" and Theodor in "Die Fermate." Like them, he, in the end, does not marry the female source of his inspiration.

In its clever blend of supernatural and everyday components, this narrative shares many features with another story set in Berlin, "Fragment aus dem Leben dreier Freunde," which appears in the first book of *Die Serapionsbrüder*. In that tale, the spirit was the spinster aunt who had been abandoned on her wedding day. In both instances, the involvement of the supernatural world had no negative repercussions. Both accounts come before the beginning of a short series of more menacing tales. "Fragment aus dem Leben dreier Freunde" appears before "Der Artushof" and "Die Bergwerke zu Falun"; "Die Brautwahl" comes before "Der unheimliche Gast" and "Das Fräulein von Scuderi." It is clear that the author is capable of strongly varying the tone and the narrative level at which he presents his notions and fears about the unseen subconscious world. He also appears to enjoy placing a relatively cheerful tale directly before accounts of a more gloomy character.

It could be said that "Die Brautwahl" qualifies as an example of the "fantastic-marvelous" in Todorov's system (even though it is also not too far from the concept of the "pure" fantastic). It is true that no direct supernatural explanations of the fantastic events and characters are directly stated to change the nature of the story at the end. But the reader, nevertheless, becomes more and more convinced of the authentic revenant status of Leonhard and Lippold as their powers are demonstrated. The reader has at first been very hesitant as to the real identity of these revenants, a reaction which is deliberately encouraged by Leonhard's own comments regarding the uncertainty of his own identity. A phrase such as "Man nennt mich" further underscores this hesitation. Despite the author's occasional use of the word "märchenhaft" the story is by no means a *Märchen* since it is firmly rooted in the real world in spite of all the fantastic events which are included.

"Die Brautwahl" offers a contrast between good supernatural forces and evil ones, and the former in the end prevail. The fantastic elements in another story in the same collection, "Vampirismus," on the other hand convey a much more dominant dark and outright ghoulish mood.

Vampirismus

"Vampirismus," "Eine Vampirgeschichte," "Eine gräßliche Geschichte" or "Hyäne" (the story is called different things in different editions and is officially untitled), was published in the last volume of *Die Serapionsbrüder* in 1821. In the frame of the collection itself, the tale is referred to by Cyprian as "eine gräßliche Geschichte." (*Werke* 8:198) The latter title may be the most suitable choice, considering the fact that the account is not technically a vampire narrative per se but could, without a doubt, be considered horrible or "gräßlich." This was an original tale directly intended for the collection. Lothar Pikulik concludes that the narrative must have been written at the beginning of the year of publication. (Pikulik 200)

"Vampirismus" tells the story of a strange marriage between a young count, Hyppolit, and a young woman of noble birth whose mother the count strongly fears but tries to tolerate. Strange rumors concerning the older woman abound even though macabre deviations such as vampirism or cannibalism are never directly stated in relation to her even though such things, as the story reveals, directly afflict her daughter. The nobleman, in the end, has to deal with the shock of facing the fact that his spouse has a less than human and clearly cannibalistic nature, something which, not unexpectedly, becomes too much of a strain on his sanity. This shocking end separates this narrative from many of Hoffmann's other tales which portray a world where evil forces ultimately are defeated and goodness is duly rewarded.

"Vampirismus" introduces a very dissimilar world in which goodness is destroyed by negative forces, no matter how much benevolence and courage virtue can muster. The young Count Hyppolit (who behaved amiably to a relative his father has apparently maltreated) as noted weds this relative's attractive but deeply troubled daughter. He attempts to assist this young woman in dealing with the horrible problems which she encounters, only to ultimately be completed destroyed for his pains. This progressive deterioration of his personality takes place on the family estate, in the midst of a familiar environment which is meticulously maintained. The tale helps to bring home, as so many accounts in *Die Serapionsbrüder* do, the closeness of satanic powers to everyday existence. Aurelie bravely attempts to fight against the fate her mother appears to have foreordained for her and continues to meet the terrible crises of her life with generosity and fortitude until the last one becomes too much for her.

The transition to this chamber of horrors appears in the frame conversation before the beginning of the bizarre narrative. Included in the conversation is a detailed discussion of actual vampires. Once again, the author (apart from giving literary examples based on Byron and Tieck) makes use of supposedly factual stories from various sources, including M. Michael Ranft's little book *Diaconi zu Nebra* (written already in 1734) which describes the existence and activities of Hungarian vampires at some length. In order to give these depictions more credibility he names names. As in the case in the section on magnetism, factual descriptions appear before a longer account. "Vampirismus," like many of the untitled tales in the collection, was apparently related to Cyprian by an acquaintance of the family.

The foregoing analysis has demonstrated that this story is very similar to other accounts without a title in regard to the factual presentations that precede it and to its connection with the extraordinary personal experiences of one of the *Serapionsbrüder*. "Vampirismus" includes many of the same motifs used elsewhere, both in the frame and in the inner stories, to indicate the existence of evil in a specific individual, such as the intensive, penetrating stare of the baroness, the cold shudders which the count feels in this woman's company, the crippling of the ability to speak, and eyes that gaze without seeing. The baroness is thus portrayed as a demonic and almost ghostlike character early in the tale. The physical description of her reinforces this impression. The old woman, with her unnaturally cold hands and lifeless eyes, also gives the count the sense of being frighteningly close to death itself:

> ... eiskalte Schauer durchbebten sein Innerstes. Er fühlte seine Hand von im Tode erstarrten Fingern umkrallt, und die große knochendürre Gestalt der Baronesse, die ihn anstarrte mit Augen ohne Sehkraft, schien ihm in den häßlich bunten Kleidern eine angeputzte Leiche. (*Werke* 8:200)

All of these manifestations signify that a higher (in this case evil) force makes its presence felt. Similar depictions exist in stories such as "Der unheimliche Gast," "Die Automate," "Der Kampf der Sänger" and "Nachricht aus dem Leben eines bekannten Mannes."

There are many clues in the flashbacks of the account that indicate that the old woman is under the direct influence of the devil. A dramatic moment is especially present when the baroness describes how the devil gained control over her during her daughter's birth, something which naturally causes Aurelie great pain. (Werke 8:208) In this context she also makes a reference to pregnancy, an allusion intended to underscore the hereditary nature of the curse which will also harm her child. Like the count in "Der unheimliche Gast," the baroness is found dead on the morning of the wedding between her daughter and the count. But, whereas the power of the count vanishes upon his death, the curse of the baroness survives her and visits itself upon Aurelie. The daughter proves to be totally in the grip of monstrous forces and ultimately physically attacks her husband with a seemingly cannibalistic intent. In his brief account of the tale, Pikulik mentions an important passage from Johann Christian Reil's *Rhapsodieen über die Anwendung der psychischen Curmethode auf Geisteszerrüttungen* (published in 1803) as a possible inspiration for Hoffmann's choice of such a grotesque scene. In this work, a pregnant woman lusts after the flesh of her husband to such a degree that she murders him and salts his flesh so that she can enjoy it for a long time. (Pikulik 202)

In its stress on the impossibility of escape from mysterious forces, this tale has a great deal in common with accounts such as "Das Fräulein von Scuderi" and "Die Bergwerke zu Falun." As with insanity and magnetism, fear can also serve as a tool that expands the consciousness of the artist, offering yet another example of the interrelatedness of the author's themes of madness, magnetism, and the spirit world in providing a stimulus for the artist as long as he can keep a safe distance. It is also worth noting that this idea of fear as an origin of creative imagination corresponds exceptionally well to the analysis of the fantastic presented by Roger Caillois and Louis Vax who both define the genre as a "game with fear."

"Vampirismus" with its emphasis on some truly terrifying motives and events and supernatural creatures provides an excellent example of this particular demarcation of the fantastic. The story with its terrifying theme also fits well into the broader delineation of the fantastic as a "brutal intrusion into everyday life of some kind of mystery" as defined by Pierre-Georges Castex. (Castex 8) The constant nearness of death reinforces that brutality.

Inge Kolke has correctly stressed the immediate and dramatic juxtaposition of death and life in the tale as exemplified by the so-called *Leichenfresser* who appear in it. These characters could be considered transitional figures between the world of the living and the world of the dead. It is only near the end of the story that the reader finds out that Aurelie is one of these bizarre and ultimately tragic individuals who consume corpses in a churchyard. Kolke also mentions the fact that the count includes a church and this particular churchyard in his domain when his castle and its surroundings are rebuilt and redesigned. He thereby violates the sharp border between life and death which the convention of his time required. (Kolke 34) But even more important is the factor that churchyards, according to tradition, attract the devil. Those living nearby therefore run the obvious risk of succumbing to a powerful demonic force bent on promoting all that is evil. This is exactly what occurs in "Vampirismus."

The existence of evil in satanic form in the tale is also directly referred to by the author, who explains certain events and phenomena as the result of the "List des Satan." (Werke 8: 208) Through the voice of baroness, he furthermore speaks of the evil spirit who is in control of Aurelia's life and is able to punish her: "... und ich wünsche selbst, daß die fürchterliche Strafe dich nicht treffen mag, die der böse Geist über dich verhängt hatte." (Werke 8:206)

Long before the dramatic end of the account, the reader is informed by the author, through various hints, that there is something seriously wrong with Aurelia. The young woman isolates herself more and more and even her husband sees her less and less. Especially significant is the information that she hardly eats anything and seems to have a direct aversion to normal human food. The mystery concerning where her nutrition comes from is only resolved in the last parts of the narrative when her cannibalistic tendencies are fully revealed.

It should be noted that, despite the depiction of more traditional vampires in the conversation among the Serapionsbrüder preceding the tale, "Vampirismus," as shown, actually inverts the idea of vampirism. The living devour the dead instead of the other way around, which would be the normal thing for a conventional blood-consuming vampire. But in spite of Hoffmann's emphasis on outright cannibalism, the theme of the direct connection between life and death and the violation of the borderline between those two states which vampirism entails remains the same.

Apart from being a good example of the fantastic as a manifestation of fear, as discussed by literary theorists such as Caillois and Vax, the narrative is also an important illustration of Todorov's concept of the "pure" fantastic. The reader's hesitation in relation to the strange occurrences in the tale remains unresolved by the end of the story, even though the shock value seems to increase the longer the story develops, and it culminates at the very end when Aurelia throws herself at her husband's chest and bites him intending to devour his flesh and immediately thereafter falls down and dies. Count Hyppolit, as a result of this horrific experience, perhaps not entirely surprisingly, loses his mind. The Todorovian concept of the continuing hesitation of the reader in relation to the text is also exemplified in "Vampirismus" by the count's own doubts regarding what he has observed at the churchyard. Has he only seen what he himself refers to as a possible "abscheuliches Traumbild?" Even though that specific question is not clearly answered, his wife's attack on him is all too real.

"Vampirismus," despite its rather obvious emphasis on pure shock value, provides an interesting example of the theme of demonic possession. The baroness is herself a devil-like character, even though she is not the devil himself. Her evil influence also ultimately destroys her child. Aurelia, as the powerless victim of diabolical forces, also connects the account with many of Hoffmann's other stories which stress the experiences of the victims of such forces rather than the actions and personality of the victimizer. Since "Vampirismus" emphasizes the role of both, it could be regarded as a transitional tale in relation to stories ("such as Die Bergwerke zu Falun") where the victims are undisputably in the forefront of attention. Women interestingly enough (as directly opposed to the devilish destructiveness of the old baroness) often play the role of potential saviors in such narratives, although they might also appear as demons in the same story. This considerable shift in the focus of the story line to the victims of evil, as compared to the interest in the diabolical characters themselves, merits a closer investigation of examples of such more victim-oriented tales.

Chapter Six

Female Saviors and Female Vampires: The Victimization of Man by Demonic Powers in "Die Bergwerke zu Falun," "Das Fräulein von Scuderi" and "Spielerglück"

Introduction

Two of Hoffmann's better known tales, "Die Bergwerke zu Falun" and "Das Fräulein von Scuderi" were both written at the end of 1818. Because of the similarities in themes they could even be considered companion pieces to each other even though the nature of the fantastic elements in them differs sharply. They both provide excellent material for a Todorovian analysis of the fantastic (even though the fantastic elements in the latter story are a lot more limited in scope than comparable components in the former). These stories both include a part of the same period of Hoffmann's works in that they are more sharply dualistic than probably at any other point in his life. The two worlds of light and darkness and their images in the double personalities of Elis Fröbom and Cardillac, contrast more harshly with each other than such components in earlier writings. The areas of confrontation are a sympathetically regarded world of reality (the Olivier-Madelon and Elis-Ulla relationship) and a mysterious dark realm nearby from which harmful characters surface (the diabolic and perilous mine in Falun and the Parisian night plagued by killers). It is noteworthy that the symbolic materials of both somber underworlds are identical: stone and metal.

Another aspect of this dualism of good and evil is presented in the brief account entitled "Spielerglück" which could be considered loosely connected with the other two tales. In "Spielerglück," the demonic forces of darkness have their impact in tempting the protagonist to gamble away his life. In this story, the question is raised (but not definitively answered) whether love and companionship are the only remedies against devilish destructiveness in general. The true nature of the female characters involved becomes significant in this regard.

Female characters indeed offer an important contrast of great importance in the stories as they are juxtaposed to represent good and evil. In "Die Bergwerke zu Falun," for instance, the angelic Ulla is sharply contrasted with the destructive "mountain queen." Positive female traits clearly dominate, on the other hand, in "Das Fräulein von Scuderi." In "Spielerglück" the contrasting effect is somewhat more vague. Because of the very transparent dualism present in "Die Bergwerke zu Falun," this tale can serve as a proper first point of departure for discussing all three narratives.

Die Bergwerke zu Falun

"Die Bergwerke zu Falun" was, as noted, written in late 1818 and published in 1819 as an original story in the third volume of *Die Serapionsbrüder*. The tale thus belongs to Hoffmann's later production. The subject of the story is based on a real event, namely an occurrence in Falun, a Swedish copper mining town, where the body of a miner, Mats Israelsson, who disappeared in 1670, was discovered in 1719 in remarkably good preservation and was recognized, it is said, by his former fiancée. This subject matter was also later treated by Hugo von Hoffmansthal in his drama *Das Bergwerk zu Falun*. Before Hoffmann, Johann Peter Hebel had depicted the event in an anecdote entitled "Unerhofftes Wiedersehen." Hoffmann himself was probably most inspired by Gotthilf Heinrich Schubert's brief version of the occurrence as he had presented it in his *Ansichten von der Nachseite der Naturwissenschaft*. (Schubert 215). From this background of documented reality, Hoffmann has created a highly romantic tale, replete with elements of unreality, fantasy and imagination. In order to fully understand how he has accomplished his narrative goals, it is necessary to know the important points of the plot.

"Die Bergwerke zu Falun" may, in some ways, appear to be a companion piece to "Der Sandmann," since both tales can be interpreted as case histories in insanity and as stories of ultimate destruction by the supernatural forces of evil. Elis Fröbom's curious account of darkness and annihilation is related from his perspective (but *not* in a first person narrative) until his death in the mine; the end of the narrative is then recounted from the point of view of his fiancée Ulla Dahlsjö. Just as in the tale of "Der Sandmann," the protagonist is annihilated either by his insanity or by powers of evil, which he perceives as pursuing him. The author has included both possibilities in this ambiguous and paradoxical story about the distressed miner who perishes in a dark Swedish mine on his wedding day before the marriage ceremony can even take place.

The protagonist Elis is portrayed as an habitually depressed loner who is suffering from anxieties and displays such erratic behavior that he is an undependable witness from the very beginning of the tale. After having returned from a lengthy voyage, he refuses to join the celebration of his fellow sailors. Due to his customary melancholy, his friends rebuke him for being a fool who wastes his time with nonsensical thoughts instead of drinking and dallying with the waterfront girls who take money in exchange for favors. One sailor, remarking that Elis is melancholy by nature, pledges to send him a girl who will get him off the bench where he is pouting.

When the young prostitute comes to Elis, he sullenly rejects her. Alone again, he gives in to his morose state of mind. He says that he wishes he were dead (thereby anticipating his dramatic death in the mine). An old miner who overhears him starts a conversation with Elis, who explains that he has just come home from a year at sea, only to learn that his mother (his last living relative) has died during his absence. The joy of his life has been to return from voyages to place money and treasures in his mother's lap and keep her company in the evenings, listening to her tell stories of the sea which she has heard from her sailor spouse. Since the mother apparently has been the only woman in his life, the reader may wonder if Elis has problems adjusting to the opposite sex.

Sensing the depressed state of mind of the young sailor, the old miner advises him to start a new life and become a miner. Directly responding to Elis' declared fear of going down into the earth, the old miner depicts the transcendental splendor of the underworld. As if induced by the fiery fancy of the miner, the young sailor feels as if he were already in the depths of the mine, with some powerful magic holding him so that he would never see daylight again: "Er fühlte seine Brust beklemmt, es war ihm, als sei er schon hinabgefahren mit dem Alten in die Tiefe, und ein mächtiger Zauber halte ihn unten fest, so daß er nie mehr das freundliche Licht des Tages schauen werde." (*Werke* 5:205)

After the old miner's departure, Elis rents a room at the inn. After having fallen asleep, he experiences a fantastic dream in which he finds himself in the mine described by the miner. When the appearance of a woman's imperial face in the subterranean world terrifies him, he hears his mother calling him from above ground. Looking up, instead of seeing his mother, he detects a beautiful young woman who is stretching her hand out to save him. Elis tells the miner, who accompanies him in his dream, to take him above. Instead of climbing up, however, he looks into the face of the majestic woman and feels himself turning into stone.

Elis wakes up screaming with the conflicting sentiments of euphoria and horror in his heart. He feels so odd that he wonders if he is still dreaming. Deciding that he is ill, he goes out into the night. Suddenly his dream returns, filling him with terror and desire as he once again stares into the face of the curious woman. His hallucinations are so commanding that the sailors who find him have to repeatedly shake him to get his attention.

At this point the reader can assume that the protagonist of the story is the victim of an uneasiness which could have a sexual basis. Moreover, it is evident that his mind is degenerating fast, since now, in addition to having delusions, he begins to hear a voice commanding him to become a miner:

Aber nun war es, als flüstre eine bekannte Stimme ihm unaufhöhrlich ins Ohr: "Was willst du noch hier? —fort! —fort—in den Bergwerken zu Falun ist deine Heimat.—Da geht alle Herrlichkeit dir auf, von der du geträumt—fort, fort nach Falun!" (*Werke* 5:208)

While the bizarre characters of his dreams pursue him, Elis constantly hears a voice instructing him to go to Falun. Believing that he discerns the old miner heading down the road in the direction of the mining town, Elis feels compelled to follow him. As the young sailor continues on the road to Falun, the miner seems to appear and disappear again and again. Being aware of the sailor's mental state, the reader might assume that the apparition of the miner is simply one more expression of the protagonist's abnormality.

Elis eventually reaches Falun and looks at the enormous mine while trembling with terror and vertigo: "Elis fühlte sich von tiefen Schauern durchbebt und was dem Seemann noch niemals geschehen, ihn ergriff der Schwindel; es war ihm, als zögen unsichtbare Hände ihn hinab in den Schlund." (*Werke* 5:211) Even though Elis feels driven by compulsion to enter the mine, he finds the fortitude to break away as he decides to leave the town the next day. But his planned departure never takes place. When he meets some miners he joins their celebration. Automatically, as if incapable of making his own decisions, he follows them as they go to a dinner party.

Upon seeing Ulla Dahlsjö, his future fiancée, at the dinner, Elis instantly identifies her with the girl in his dream who stretched out her hand to save him and concludes that the dream may have a more profound message, which includes Ulla. Curiously, Elis feels sad, wishing once again he were dead, since now he is convinced that he will die of love and desire for Ulla.

Because it would entail living in the same house as Ulla, Elis chooses to become a miner, informing Ulla's father, Pehrson Dahlsjö about his decision. The work in the mine is definitely not good for the protagonist's health, since the hot vapors almost choke him. One day, as Elis works in the deepest part of the mine, he hears a strange knocking sound that seems to come from even deeper. It is possible to believe that Elis simply hallucinates in this situation, in part due to lack of oxygen.

A black shadow, which proves to be the old miner, appears. Elis hears the old man inform him that he will never marry Ulla. Reminding the main character that he is only working in the mine in order to marry her, the miner warns him that such deportment offends the Mountain Queen who, if infuriated, may throw Elis into the abyss. The old man disappears as mysteriously as he had appeared.

A foreman later informs the distraught Elis that he has seen the legendary miner Torbern, who is in league with the secret powers that rule in the depths of the earth. Torbern, killed in a mining accident on St. John's day in 1687, has reportedly been seen by other miners since then.

Deeply anxious, Elis returns home, only to find another man holding the hand of his beloved Ulla. Being completely devastated, he enters the mine at night. If a party of miners led by Pehrson Dahlsjö had not searched for him, Elis' destiny might have already been sealed at this point. Instead, the searchers find him standing rigid against the cold rock, dreaming of the Queen of the underworld.

When Ulla's father gets Elis safely back home again, he explains that he was upset with Elis because he had not asked to marry his daughter and that he had only played a trick on him by saying that his daughter was to marry another man. In a sense, Elis is pushed into a marriage just as he was pushed into becoming a miner. On one level, Elis is very happy about Ulla becoming his spouse. But this exhilaration is short-lived. He becomes more and more distant, often staring into space, which makes Ulla realize that something is wrong with him.

Even though Ulla demands an explanation for his behavior, Elis is incapable of giving one. Since he appears to be ill, he stays home from work for several days. He later returns to the mine and becomes so engrossed in his work that he forgets his fiancée and her father. Elis still visits Ulla, but whenever she talks about their love and future happiness, he changes the subject and talks about the mine. He tells Ulla and the foreman about the rich veins which he has found there. But upon looking the latter two can only detect pure rock. He laughingly informs them that only he can understand the secret writing which the Mountain Queen has written on the rock. The foreman, puzzled by this bizarre talk, blames Torbern for having bewitched Elis. Pehrson Dahlsjö, however, asserts that Elis' problems must be caused by love.

On the day of his wedding, St. John's day, Elis tells his intended bride that he must go down into the mine to get her a wedding present, an almandine, the existence of which has been revealed to him during the night. Disregarding the pleas of Ulla, Elis enters the mine and vanishes in a cave-in, thereby fulfilling the death wish previously expressed.

If the tale had ended with the protagonist's disappearance, the reader could have concluded that it had been a case history of insanity. But the account does not end here. The reader cannot simply lay the story aside convinced in his belief that Elis was simply insane. Fifty years later, on St. John's day, the day Elis was to have been married and the day on which Torbern had been killed, a peculiar occurrence takes place. In a deep hole, some miners discover the petrified body of a young miner. Even the flowers and the wedding suit he wears are perfectly preserved. An old woman arrives on the scene. It is Ulla, who has come to the mine every St. John's day since Elis vanished. Recognizing his body, she exclaims that Torbern had told her that she would see her beloved again. Ulla dies on Elis' body, which falls into ashes. The remains of both are taken to the church where they were to have been married.

At the end of the story, the reader still retains a strong sense of ambiguity. It is simply very hard to say whether the visions of the main character are genuine or pure hallucinations. The mysterious ghost of the old miner is a case in point. If Torbern really exists, that is, really is what the legend portrays, then he must be considered a true fantastic figure within the context of the narrative. If, on the other hand, the old miner can be irrefutably demonstrated as nothing more than myth and a projection of the hallucinations of the protagonist, then a significant supernatural element in the story disappears. There is, however, a third possibility. If each of the ghost's appearances is adeptly made ambiguous, then we have a narrative of uncertain fantastic content. Each element which would attest to a fantastic event is in turn modified by opposing evidence. This technique is often used in this tale in order to underscore its ambiguity. Especially important in this regard is the absence of independent testimony to inexplicable happenings. One example of this is the fact that at no time does a third person in the account see Elis together with the old miner. This narrative technique accomplishes major uncertainty on the part of the reader. It could be concluded that any narrative statement resting on the perception of one character alone is subject to scrutiny for unreliability. This simple narrative method depends on what is *not* stated. This makes Torbern's role even more ambiguous. When Elis starts his long trek from Gothenburg to Falun, he eventually notices the miner in front of him. Hoffmann's presentation of this contact is revealing as to his narrative technique:

> In der Tat sah er auch manchmal, vorzüglich wenn der Weg ihm ungewiss werden wollte, den Alten, wie er aus einer Schlucht, aus dickem Gestripp, aus dunklem Gestein plötzlich hervortrat, und vor ihm ohne sich umzuschauen daherschritt, dann aber schnell wieder verschwand. (*Werke* 5:209–210)

The author's use of the phrase "in der Tat" is important. Does this mean that the narrator actually states that the protagonist observes a real ghost? This is not necessarily the case. But the formulation makes it important to address the issue of the narrator as a reliable conveyer of information. In the case of Hoffmann's production this is a significant problem since the author frequently places ambiguity on the narrator himself. In this story, this ambiguity appears several times, as for instance in the depiction of Elis' state of mind in Gothenburg: "Drei Tage trieb sich Elis Fröbom in den Straßen von Göteborg umher, unaufhörlich verfolgt von den wunderlichen Gebilden seines Traumes, unaufhörlich gemahnt von der unbekannnten Stimme". (*Werke* 5:208.) This is simply a portrayal of the mood and thoughts of the main character. The description says nothing regarding the reality of the voice; either that it is a hallucination or that it is a genuine voice of a fantastic force. The reader is thus left with at least the possibility of a supernatural explanation.

The final part of the narrative gives further credence to a supernatural explanation of the strange occurrences described. Ulla explains her presence at the mine by informing people that Torbern had consoled her by telling her that she would see Elis again. Since Ulla hears and believes the old miner and his prophecy that she would be reunited with her intended bridegroom, the story of Elis would seem corroborated. The innocent Ulla has seen the ghost as well, and that would appear to be an independent confirmation of the old miner's existence. The reader would therefore be justified in believing in the protagonist's claim that he is persecuted by supernatural forces which in the end annihilate him. On closer consideration, however, it must be remembered that the legend of Torbern was well-known in Falun and one other miner believed Torbern directly responsible for the insanity of the protagonist. The skeptical reader could also legitimately believe that the bride-to-be became unbalanced by the cruel shock of the death of her betrothed on their wedding day and his talk of Torbern, so that she hallucinated the latter's visit to her. It was thus pure coincidence that she was at the mine when Elis' body was returned to the surface. Ulla's testimony should therefore be regarded as questionable. A supernatural as well as a natural interpretation would be plausible when one keeps such factors in mind. Irony is a further element which stresses this ambiguous nature of the account.

Irony is the structural principle of this paradoxical tale, which simultaneously contains two distinctly different meanings; therefore the story should be read in two ways. The text, deliberately ambiguous, demonstrates that the protagonist was annihilated by his own insanity while at the same time being the victim of evil powers outside himself. Hoffmann, a master of ambiguity, has created in "Die Bergwerke zu Falun" a completely ambivalent narrative, as well as a superb manifestation of Romantic irony.

The Romantic irony present in this story has extremely tragic connotations. A main theme of the tale is one of demonic seduction, which originates in secret powers. Elis becomes a victim of these powers, perhaps primarily because he has lost his mother, and therefore much of the meaning in his life. His care for her had been the most important thing in his life. It could even be said that he finally loses his childhood and the natural connection with his origins. Further clues to the nature of Hoffmann's irony can also be found in the conversation of the *Serapionsbrüder* surrounding the story.

Going beyond the text itself is thus helpful in addressing interpretative problems considering the nature of the events of the story. Some hints to a reasonable interpretation of the narrative can be found in the frame conversation directly succeeding the story. One of the members of the circle, Cyprian, who frequently expresses his fascination for aberrant states of consciousness, makes this comment, which appears to apply especially to the protagonist of the account: "Wie oft stellten Dichter Menschen, welche auf irgendeine entsetzliche Weise untergehen, als im ganzen Leben mit sich entzweit, als von unbekannten finstren Mächten befangen dar." (*Werke* 5:230) This observation intimates that Elis simply lacked the necessary perceptiveness and knowledge which would have made it possible for him to resist the impact of menacing outside powers.

Cyprian attempts to underscore his argument by mentioning that he himself has been acquainted with individuals who suddenly appeared pursued by satanic powers, whose character was entirely altered by these experiences. Within a short time some terrible occurrence had torn them from their normal lives. (Werke 5:230) This comment is, as Vickie Ziegler has correctly stressed, reminiscent of a device that the author utilized in the beginning frame and that one finds repeated throughout the work; personal experiences corroborate material derived from poetic imagination. (Ziegler 161) Cyprian's depiction of personal friends might as well refer to the ill-fated main character of "Die Bergwerke zu Falun." Another essential component which adds credibility to the story of Elis Fröbom is the direct reference to Schubert's account of the authentic event in Falun a hundred years earlier. (*Werke* 5:229) Ottmar's mentioning of Schubert's work is the first definite one within the collection. Schubert has influenced the tale in various ways. This scientist-philosopher was convinced that dreams could be prophetic and that in changed states of consciousness much about the future could be learned. Not all premonitions, however, are of a healthy nature. Schubert expresses this idea in the following way: "Der Blick in das zukünftige, die Gabe der Vorahnungen, ist der menschlichen Natur nicht fremd. Doch giebt es eben sowohl eine von kranker und falscher als eine von gesunder und wahrhaft echter Art." (Schubert 90) Such less than positive revelations are associated with demonism. An evil force will often exert an exceptional amount of control over an individual who has these type of visions. Schubert then compares such abnormal states with somnambulism. (Schubert 94)

Even though these discussions clearly hint at the later debate on magnetism, they are also applicable to the role of Torbern and the obscure mountain queen in Fröbom's story and they connect with Cyprian's comments about people under the control of detrimental dreams and peculiar external powers. Ensuing tales in the collection address this theme, especially in relation to artists such as Heinrich von der Ofterdingen in "Der Kampf der Sänger." Torbern-like figures, with supernatural powers over their victims, surface in stories like "Der unheimliche Gast."

Another force which grips Elis is his fatal attraction to the riches of the mine. Not until he pays allegiance to the mysterious queen does he become entirely entranced by the subterranean realm. Then he can think of little else but the splendors of the depth and the remarkable treasures concealed there. It appears to Elis as if his real better self is with the mountain queen and the city above the mine is dark and strange. (*Werke* 5:224)

Fascination with metals is something which Schubert addresses in a chapter on animal magnetism. He is convinced that metals not only attract but also magnetize anyone who is susceptible to them. One of the most important areas which shows the closest relationship to animal magnetism is that of precious metals. (Schubert 355–56) Schubert thus implies that it is conceivable that a metal can act as a magnetizer. This characteristic of metals assists in explaining why Fröbom, like Angelika and Moritz in "Der unheimliche Gast," appears sometimes not in his right mind. It is important to note that the protagonist believes that he alone has the knowledge of where the richest veins in the mine are. This could be regarded as a reflection of Schubert's assertion that only a magnetized individual can perceive the presence of metals.

The expected discovery of immense riches, of course, pertains to the future. But the past also plays a major part in the story. In his dreams, the ghost Torbern constantly reminds Elis of his past, and he recognizes parallels between his current and former life, in other words, he is confronted with many déjà vu experiences.

There are also definite parallels between this world and the world below. In Elis' dreams, these two worlds flow together and it is not possible to find clear boundaries between them. When Elis' mind gets increasingly darker, so does the physical world around him. The sky, for instance, disappears behind total darkness.

But at the same time, the realm of the underworld down in the mines stands as a sharp contrast to the world of everyday reality. The ghost Torbern presents the realm of the Mountain Queen as one of great wonders and great beauty. This is one image of this mysterious realm offered by the author: "Er blickte in die paradiesischen Gefilde der herrlichsten Metallbäume und Pflanzen, an denen die Früchte, Blüten und Blumen feuerstrahlende Steine hingen." (*Werke* 5:222)

The realm of metals and stones had a special fascination to many romantic writers. Such material riches can, of course, also be found in mountains as well as far down in mines. Ludwig Tieck's story *Der Runenberg*, for instance, as among others Elisabeth Wright has pointed out, forms an interesting parallell to Hoffmann's story. One reason for the romantic fascination with this topic is that the realm of metals and stones is deep, bizarre, inhuman and a sharp contrast to this world of plants, animals and human beings. This in reality lifeless realm, reflects the original state of the world and the secrets of creation itself are concealed there. The great paradox in Hoffmann's narrative is that this inorganic world actually comes to life, and thereby definitely surpasses the boundaries of reality.

Elis' experiences in both worlds are described in sequences which immediately suggest the logic of a dream: the space which contains him shifts and changes, it is peopled by strange organisms which grow and develop like figures in a mannerist painting. Therefore, the nature of the temptations Elis encounters in his dreams tend to change in nature.

At the same time, however, it is possible to find some constant features relating to what tempts him. The predominance of sea imagery is important in this regard. The place where Elis' first dream occurs is the port of Gothenburg. Hoffmann gives his settings a local realistic habitation. It is worth noting that the sea is an image long since associated with the idea of a life force, an image that turns up time and time again in myths, fairy tales, visions and dreams.

In the initial part of his first dream, the protagonist feels as if he is sailing away on a ship, looking up at the dark ceiling of the sky. But then he looks down, and the bottom of the sea appears to solidify into a crystal base and what was sky turns into the rock of a huge cavern. Organic life is suddenly surging about him, thus suggesting the bottom of the sea again, where fantastic organisms might thrive. The fantastic element is immediately evident, as the thrusting plants turn out to be of metal, thus a direct parallel to his later dreams and visions. Here the connotation of glittering metal is free from associations of desire for material wealth. It rather belongs to a collocation of words pertaining to light, words such as crystal, white, light, sparkling and glimmering. These words are used to heighten the effect of the weird and the wonderful.

These elements of the story can also be seen in light of the so-called *Naturphilosophie*, of the early nineteenth century and especially the ideas of Friedrich Schelling. According to this philosophy, nature is regarded as consisting of one harmonious whole, with no distinctions between organic and inorganic life. Schelling describes metals as substances bearing the visible signs of the transition between the stone world and the plant world. Schubert, being a disciple of this philosopher, states this idea in the following way: "Das ganze Reich der Metalle, scheint an der Grenze der beiden Welten zu sein". (Schubert 201)

This evolutionary process also appears to be transpiring in the dreams of the protagonist in "Die Bergwerke zu Falun". Yet clearly Hoffmann's depictions go beyond that of nineteenth century *Naturphilosophie*. The imagery is developed with what could be called metaphysical wit in both its senses: the original meaning, of pertaining to another world, and the literary meaning as derived from the metaphysical poets. The latter sense is applicable here because there are images which are so far-fetched as to merit being called conceits. The strange plants rising from the depths turn out to be the progeny of countless maidens who embrace each other.

The etymological word play of this part of the story links the fertility of the plants to that of the maidens as part of one evolutionary process. The almost whimsical note struck here, is further developed in that the organ from which the plants sprout is the heart, the center of the emotions as of life. Procreation and fertility are thus taken out of the biological sphere and spiritualized.

A conflict arises between this surge towards life and activity, and the desire for freedom from tension and worries. Elis initially sees a state of primal bliss. But he also experiences the total abandonment of the self in the characters of Torbern and the powerful woman (that is the mountain queen). Hence he feels conflicting emotions of rapture, bliss, anguish and outright fear. The focus of the story is thus firmly based on the plight of a man, beckoned and even tortured by two different worlds which cannot be reconciled. The depths of the earth flow together with the depths of his soul.

The romantic sensibility and subjectivity of the story does not stop with a first-person experience. The seemingly objective pronoun "it" represents the subconscious dimension. What is particularly noteworthy in this story, as opposed to most of Hoffmann's stories, is that the external physical world could have saved the protagonist from destructive demonic forces. His inner thoughts are what inevitably draw him into the realm of darkness. In most of Hoffmann's stories, the opposite tends to be the case. The physical world is normally the great threat. But not so in this story in which the author has chosen a different approach.

One must, in this context, also remember yet another aspect of Elis' fate, the strongly erotic dimension of the tale. The Mountain Queen offers a strong erotic attraction, and in her subterrestrial realm many young women, referred to as virgins, have the same effect on Elis. This is also a sharp contrast to his "pure" love for Ulla, his fiancée. The Mountain Queen also directly leads Elis to his death. When he is discovered he is found embracing a rock, presumably in his own mind the of body of mountain queen. The reader knows this because this is the position in which he is reported the last time the narrator mentions him as a living person.

Another important element of the tale is Elis' search for the wonderful almandin, key to the meaning of life, a meaning that has been lost to him after the death of his mother. Elis believes that the Mountain Queen has this key in her hands, but it is never quite clear whether he is right or not; another example of the ambiguous nature of the tale.

The tragic end of the narrative raises the question of whether or not the author himself believes that life has a real meaning and if he believes that death can be a salvation. The former question cannot be easily addressed on the basis of this text. The latter does not appear to be the case for Elis, who is seduced by demonic forces. Love in real life would have been his redemption, but this is not to be. It is therefore difficult to avoid the conclusion that the story strongly reflects a fundamental pessimism which is to be found in many of Hoffmann's stories. "Die

Bergwerke zu Falun" thus fits well into a more general tendency in the author's view of existence, despite the somewhat different perspective on life offered here.

Die Bergwerke zu Falun is also rather typical of the writer's production from a Todorovian point of view. Todorov's strong emphasis on ambiguity and reader hesitation is rarely as well exemplified as in this, at times, somewhat obscure narrative. The story retains this quality unaltered also at the very end which makes it an excellent illustration of Todorov's "pure fantastic." A solution bringing the tale within the subgenres of the "fantastic-uncanny" or "fantastic-marvelous" is never offered. Another narrative with some fantastic content that would be categorized quite differently in the Todorovian system is *Das Fräulein von Scuderi*.

Das Fräulein von Scuderi

Hoffmann's writing of "Das Fräulein von Scuderi" was begun in March of 1818 and the tale was completed in the fall of the same year. It was first published in 1819 in *Taschenbuch für das Jahr 1820*. It was made a part of *Die Serapionsbrüder* (volume three) the following year.

This complex narrative depicts how late one night an intense knocking is heard on the door of a certain Parisian lady of noble origin, Magdaleine Scuderi. Her manservant is not there and the apprehensive maid, Martiniere, is only too well aware of the horrible crimes, robbery and murder, which have been terrorizing Paris for several months. From an upstairs window she talks briefly with a man standing at the door, and, determining that he may actually be seeking sanctuary, she admits an excited, frantically agitated youth, whose simplicity and honesty are disarming, but she sternly rejects the request to wake up her mistress despite his pleading and even his threats. Then, placing a small casket in her hands, the young man rushes from the house. At this point, the manservant, Baptiste, returns; he had been detained by the police and had been released only when the chief of police finally had recognized him. As he approached the house, he had seen a cloaked figure, with a dagger in his hand, rushing away from the door. Both Baptiste and Martiniere are convinced that some horrible plot has been conceived against their mistress; at first they intend to throw the casket into the Seine, but then agree instead to inform Miss de Scuderi about the events of the morning.

After this introductory scene, created to arouse interest and tension, the author pauses in the main narrative to give a lengthy account of the fear that has plagued Paris; the invention of a mysterious poison which kills its victims without leaving a trace, and the following wave of shocking murders, creating horror everywhere and setting even members of families in fear of one another, since no one appears to be safe. Then, coming closer to the narrative itself, Hoffmann depicts the chain of baffling murders on the streets at night, and the establishment of a special police unit, up to this point foiled in its efforts to trace the murderer or murderers. Desgrais, a lieutenant of the police force, has in fact seen such a crime committed only a few meters from his place of watching. A cavalier walking along the street was struck down by an assailant who appeared to come from nowhere. Desgrais attempted to catch him, but the mysterious aggressor disappeared in front of him, as if he had melted into a long wall: other police officers emerged but found no clues to the mystery.

It has been noted that those particularly marked for the assassin's dagger have been young cavaliers carrying gifts—primarily jewels—to their ladies. An appeal for protection is sent to the king by some of these gallants. Mlle de Scuderi, an intimate friend of Madame de Maintenon and much appreciated by the king himself, happens to be present when the petition is read; her remark on the occasion is soon quoted all over the city: "Un amant qui craint les voleurs n'est point digne d'amour." (*Werke* 7:176)

On the morning after the occurrences described at the beginning Mlle de Scuderi hears the report from her servants and with a great deal of apprehension opens the casket, to find jeweled bracelets and a necklace of splendid craftsmanship, but she is frightened and humiliated but the accompanying note from the "Invisible One," thanking her for the sentiments in her comment quoted above. Mlle de Scuderi immediately goes to the apartment of Madame de Maintenon, and in seeing the jewel the former recognizes the workmanship of Cardillac, the most talented maker of jewels in the French capital or even in the whole of Europe. Summoned to explain the puzzle, he acknowledges his work and explains that he has missed these jewels from his workshop, but he is curiously flustered and elusive in his manner, persisting in his idea that Mlle de Scuderi, whom he has admired for a long time, should keep the jewels, and in spite of her protests he rushes from the apartment, leaving the casket in her hand.

A few months later, as Mlle de Scuderi's carriage is crossing the Pont Neuf, an excited, impulsive youth elbows his way through the crowd and throws a note into her lap. Mlle de Scuderi's maid faints, recognizing in him the strange nocturnal visitor who brought the casket. The note begs Mlle de Scuderi to return the jewels to Cardillac at once in order to prevent serious repercussions. Circumstances stop her from doing so for a several days, and on finally coming to Cardillac's home, she finds the street crowded and in a commotion. The house itself is under guard by the police. Cardillac has been murdered, and his assistant Olivier, the fiancé of his daughter Madelon, has been arrested as the perpetrator of the crime. He turns out to be the young man of the casket episode. Moved by sympathy for the lamenting girl, who maintains that her lover is innocent, Mlle de Scuderi brings her to her own house.

After this incident, a police investigation ensues, including the expanded probing into the conditions of the murder victim's household and the questioning of the suspected malefactor who is under arrest. Circumstantial evidence against him is strong, and it is natural to interpret the situation in such a way as to provide a motive. It appears clear that Olivier is not disclosing everything which he knows and this testifies against him. Even Mlle de Scuderi hesitates in her opinion and against the sentiments of her heart starts to believe in Olivier's guilt. The outcome of her first interview with the prisoner is far from acceptable, but in the second, which he himself asks for, the accused, who now risks torture and possibly death, wholeheartedly puts his fate into her hand.

Olivier reveals his true identity. He is the son of an old friend and protégée of Mlle de Scuderi whom she has held in her arms in his childhood. In Geneva, where his parents had gone, he had been the apprentice of a goldsmith and had become a master craftsman; and had then turned to Cardillac, to find a place with the foremost artist in the field. Eventually he discovered the secret of his colleague. Cardillac's love of precious jewels, the product of his creative mastery, had become an obsession, a limitless passion; now he cannot bear to part with them and comes up with innumerable excuses to delay the delivery of an order; once in the hands of another person, they form an irresistible lodestone inciting him to robbery and murder. In view of this insanity, he refuses orders from those whom he personally honors. To curb his master's demented obsession, Olivier has attempted the experiment of getting these particular jewels into the hands of Mlle de Scuderi, being aware of Cardillac's high regard for her. The plan works for a time. His master is quiet and collected, but Olivier notes an increased tendency toward mental disquiet, of frenzied agitation, and therefore delivers the note demanding the immediate return of the jewels. On the night of the fatal tragedy the young assistant has followed Cardillac, leaving the house by a secret door in the garden wall and witnessing the attack upon his master and colleague. Olivier then brings the dying man home. He admits to his own guilt in keeping silent for the sake of Cardillac's daughter. He has not been able to ruin her happiness by disclosing the crimes of her father.

In the meantime the real killer of Cardillac tells his story to Mlle de Scuderi. A young aristocrat, Comte de Miossens, had ordered jewels from the famous goldsmith but grew suspicious as a result of Cardillac's question as to the address of his lady and the time he intended to visit her. He then went over the accounts of earlier homicides, noting the kind of dagger thrust used, and placed a piece of armor under his doublet. Cardillac's blow was therefore averted, giving the Comte an instant advantage; in the struggle that follows he kills his assailant. For personal reasons, he does not want his action known, but is disturbed at the thought that an innocent man may suffer as a result of his actions.

In making his confession to Mlle de Scuderi, Olivier still insists that for the sake of Cardillac's daughter her father's crimes must not become known. The police officials to whom Mlle. de Scuderi can now disclose the whole story cannot honor her request. They cannot disregard the demands of justice or overlook Olivier's culpability in hiding the knowledge he has possessed for so long. Only the king is able to intervene and he does so. Olivier and Madelon are married, but after the horrible experiences of the last few months, Olivier can not stand the thought of remaining in Paris; instead, he returns with his bride to Geneva.

This is, in brief, what takes place in the incredible tale of the master artist and murderer Cardillac. The narrative has many features in common with the traditional detective story and it could easily be argued that this account is an usually early example of this later so popular genre. The mysterious murders themselves are, of course, the most obvious examples of features typical of a detective story. Another element of particular importance is, as Richard Alewyn has pointed out in his essay "Ursprung des Detektivromans," the existence of an innocent person under strong suspicion (Olivier). As a contrast to this character one finds a guilty person who for the longest time is considered absolutely innocent of any crime. The fact that an outsider rather than the police solves the case also often occurs in typical examples of the genre.[1]

But *Das Fräulein von Scuderi* is more than a traditional tale of mystery and detection. The story also contains fantastic components. First of all, it could be maintained that the atmosphere of the account itself is rather fantastic. The single fantastic event portrayed in detail in the tale reinforces this sense of unreality until the end when a natural explanation is presented by one of the characters. This fantastic event is ultimately complemented by a fantastic theory intended to explain the murders through the eyes of the murderer himself. But the fantastic event early in the story sets the stage for all other fantastic aspects of this narrative.

Das Fräulein von Scuderi includes one such decisive occurrence which presents the rational reader with what appears to be the rationally incomprehensible. Desgrais, an administrator of the Parisian police, explains to his colleagues the attempted capture of the killer (only later discovered to be Cardillac). The author, through this depiction of the event, establishes a narrative atmosphere imbued with the fantastic. This scene is presented with conscientious attention to any conceivable rational objection:

> Im Mondesschimmer erkenne ich den Marquis de la Fare. Ich konnt ihn da erwarten, ich wußte, wo er fünfzehn Schritte vor mir springt der Mensch auf die Seite in den Schatten und verschwindet durch die Mauer." Verschwindet?—Durch die Mauer?—Seid ihr rasend," ruft La Regnie, indem er zwei Schritte zurücktritt und die Hände zusammenschlägt. (Werke 7:173)

But Desgrais has an uncompromising response to the natural disbelief of his superiors:

> Nennt mich, gnädiger Herr, immerhin einen Rasenden, einen törenden Geisterseher, aber es ist nicht anders als wie ich es Euch erzähle. Erstarrt stehe ich vor der Mauer, als mehrere Häscher atemlos herbeikommen; mit ihnen der Marquis de La Fare, der sich aufgerafft, den blossen Degen in der Hand. (*Werke* 7:173)

The policeman continues to depict how others join the remarkable chase:

> Wir zünden die Fackeln an, wir tappen an die Mauer hin und her; keine Spur einer Türe, eines Fensters, einer Öffnung. Es ist eine steinerne Hofmauer, die sich an ein Haus lehnt, in dem Leute wohnen, gegen die auch nicht die leiseste Verdacht aufkommt. (*Werke* 7:173)

Desgrais himself offers the following assessment after having presented this colorful description of the event: "Der Teufel selbst ist es, der uns foppt." (*Werke* 7:173)

It is important to note the skeptical reaction of the superiors of this official to his story since they represent the reader's own incredulity. The attempt to anticipate reasonable explanations of the mysterious disappearance is also of fundamental importance since it underscores the fantastic nature of the occurrence: "keine Spur einer Türe, eines Fensters, einer Öffnung." (*Werke* 7:173)

With this one incident the presumably fantastic character of the tale is firmly validated. The illusion is maintained until Olivier, much later in the account, illuminates the reader as to what really took place at the stone wall. As already noted, this is the only purely fantastic occurrence in the story and it turns out to have a rational explanation revealed at the end of the story.

The narrative stands with this one seemingly fantastic incident contributing to the profound tension which is unique to the contravention of familiar reality. Since *Das Fräulein von Scuderi* is a rather lengthy tale it could be questioned whether or not the incident at the stone wall is really necessary for the consistency and harmony of the plot as a whole. When one looks more closely at this event, it is noticeable how Olivier's depiction of the wall clearly differs from the description offered by the policeman. Olivier portrays the stone wall in the following way:

An Cardillacs Haus in der Straße Nicaise schließt sich eine hohe Mauer mit Blenden und alten, halb zerstückelten Steinbildern darin. Dicht bei einem solchen Steinbilde stehe ich in einer Nacht und sehe hinauf nach den Fenstern des Hauses, die in den Hof gehen, den die Mauer einschließt. (*Werke* 7:204)

He continues:

Ich drücke mich an das Steinbild, in die Blende hinein, doch entsetzt pralle ich zurück, als ich einen Gegendruck fühle, als sei das Bild lebendig geworden. In dem dämmernden Schimmer der Nacht gewahre ich nun, daß der Stein sich langsam dreht, und hinter demselben eine finstere Gestalt hervorschlüpft, die leisen Trittes die Straße hinabgeht. Ich springe an das Steinbild heran, es steht wie zuvor dicht an der Mauer. (Werke 7:205)

Desgrais, on the other hand, strongly maintained that there was no trace of a door, a window or any kind of opening. Has he simply ignored the statue niches? This is definitely not the case. The policeman even returned in daylight to examine the wall more closely. It is the writer of the story who deceives the reader. It is hard to answer the question whether this omission on Hoffmann's part is conscious or accidental. But if it is assumed that it is a deliberate contradiction in the depiction of a seemingly supernatural event, it seems natural to conclude that its purpose might be to emphasize the entirely subjective nature of the fantastic elements in this account. This would also be the most important reason why the chase of the elusive murderer at this point is described entirely through the eyes of individual witnesses rather than through the eyes of the main narrator. In this context, it should be noted that most significant events in the story are presented in the first rather than the third person, thereby strengthening the distancing effect on the part of the narrator.

The subjectivity of the tale, as well as its component of obvious visual illusion which is intended to deceive both characters in the story and the reader, clearly places *Das Fräulein von Scuderi* in one of Todorov's subcategories, namely the "fantastic-uncanny." But it should nonetheless be remembered that the fantastic theory offered by Cardillac is never rebuffed by the author or even by any character in the story. The question concerning the real motive for the murders gives a certain aura of mystery to the end of the account even though a logical explanation has been presented with regards to the most fantastic event in the story.

This is where the issue of the pre-natal miseries of Cardillac's mother comes into the picture. The killer's creative pathology is explained through a reference to the superstition of the day, namely the idea that the experiences and inclinations of Cardillac's mother during her pregnancy determine in detail the son's character as well as his obsessions (in this case a fixation with "Edelsteine"). This is a direct parallell to Elis Fröbom's tireless quest for the "Almandin."

This theory of inherited obsessive behavior, repeated in detail by the child of an equally obsessive parent, appears fantastic (at least at the time of the writing of the story which clearly predates any science of genetics) and also appears to be intended to at least modify the strict rationalism which the logical explanation to the sole fantastic event of the tale entails. But *Das Fräulein von Scuderi* nevertheless is logically placed in the subcategory of the fantastic-uncanny since the Todorovian system primarily emphasizes fantastic occurrences rather than fantastic theories or notions such as supernatural atmosphere.

Spielerglück

The short tale "Spielerglück" first appeared in *Urania* in 1820, and became a part of the third volume of Hoffmann's last collection that same year. The narrative has received substantially less attention than many other stories in *Die Serapionsbrüder* but again can approached within a Todorovian framework.

The main theme in "Spielerglück" is introduced by the relating of a story which is presented to the main character, Baron Siegfried. This story within a story is told by a mysterious stranger who depicts how the compulsive urge to gamble can ruin a man. The enigmatic stranger narrates the tale of Chevalier de Menars (who is in fact none other than himself) and his stormy marriage to Angela Vertua. Menars is at first lucky in gambling, but the dangerous habit ultimately destroys him as a person as well as his once happy life with Angela.

Not only does the depiction of how up-and-coming young gentlemen self-destruct through gambling fulfill the function of an impassioned plea to avoid this habit, (a characterization which is made significant through constant reiteration); it also suggests the schemes of an invisible, merciless force. The narrator alludes to this force on repeated occasions as "satanic." (*Werke* 7:242, 245) The devil's control over his victims in this type of cases is further underscored when Vertua, the protagonist's father-in-law, after having abandoned the habit of gambling several times, perishes in his passion for the dice, completely refusing confession and absolution from the priest. His daughter Angela justifiably fears that her spouse may revert to his old bad habits.

Angela is an idealized picture of a true female savior. She is portrayed as a pure, virtuous and selfless young woman. Even her family name is a direct allusion to the concept of virtue. She closely resembles other redemptive female characters such as Ulla Dahlsjö in "Die Bergwerke zu Falun." Her first appearance in a white nightdress (the color of innocence) and her speech to her desperate father further stress her redemptive traits. Vertua has already implied such an interpretation of her character, since he has told his son-in-law about how Angela's mother saved him from death. As a result of Vertua's abuse of his loyal spouse, whom he learned to truly love only a short time before her death, he gives up gambling, This parallel between Angela and her mother is also emphasized when Vertua directly states that his daughter is the image of her mother. (*Werke* 7:252)

But even Angela's excellent qualities at first have only a minor effect on her husband. In the end, however, the impact of her virtue prevails. After imploring her spouse to cease his involvement with gambling, Angela passes away, but she is still able to save her mate, even in death. When Menars discovers her lifeless body in her bed, after he has gambled her away to her former admirer, he gives up gambling permanently. After this tragic event, the grief stricken man instead attempts to save others from his own fate.

There are, as Ziegler also has pointed out, two types of gamblers in "Spielerglück," the one for whom the play of coincidence is the game itself, its seeming connection with extrasensory forces, appears to be the alluring facet of this activity, and the second who simply has an appetite for potential material riches. (Ziegler 246) Even though the sources are separate, the ultimate result, emotional and financial self-destruction, is identical in either case. Menars has seen this in himself as well as in his father-in-law. The addicted gambler is similar to a man like the murderer Cardillac in that he cannot feel the measure of the wrong the he does to others. The possession by an apparent supernatural force leads to a dehumanizing of the individual soul. A triumph of evil is therefore made possible. The supposition that such total control over other human beings was conceivable, whatever the source of this control might be, truly terrified the author as well as many other individuals of this period.

"Spielerglück" should not primarily be considered a typical fantastic story when it is analyzed from a Todorovian point of view. The demonic influence so vividly depicted in the tale is mysterious and appears to have at least a supernatural element in it. But no actual event in the narrative is necessarily totally inexplicable from the point of view of natural logic despite the occasionally supernatural atmosphere. "Spielerglück" is therefore an example of an account with the "borderline" fantastic content which Todorov has referred to as "uncanny."

More directly and unquestionably fantastic are typical Todorovian themes of "the other" such as ghosts, demons and vampires. It is well-known that Hoffmann's production includes a substantial amount of such material and it is for this reason a natural object of study when one approaches the issue of this author's close relationship with the fantastic in literature.

Chapter Seven
Ghosts, Ghouls and Automatons: "Ein Fragment aus dem Leben dreier Freunde," "Eine Spukgeschichte," "Der Artushof" and "Die Automate"

Introduction

Hoffmann's tales, apart from describing the destructive influence of evil powers on everyday life, while occasionally even letting the devil himself appear in person, also often include indisputably supernatural creatures such as ghosts. These elements correspond well to Todorov's emphasis on the definition of the fantastic as something which usually includes so-called "themes of the other" as exemplified by supernatural characters, be they ghosts, werewolves or vampires. The same components also fit perfectly into the very similar delineation of the genre by Louis Vax who, as noted previously, strongly stresses these features of the fantastic: "Un conte fantastique, c'est une histoire de vampire, de revenant, de loup-garou ..." (*Séduction* 308)

The fantastic stories written by an author who, after all, has often been referred to as "Gespenster-Hoffmann," approach such supernatural creatures in various ways. Hoffmann's depiction of ghosts can, at times, be quite lighthearted and at other times much more menacing. "Ein Fragment aus dem Leben dreier Freunde" exemplifies the former type and "Eine Spukgeschichte" represents the more somber category of tales. A bizarre account such as "Die Automate" is in many ways unique. But the more detached style of "Ein Fragment aus dem Leben dreier Freunde" (despite its somewhat atypical nature) can be a good starting point for an examination of the author's portrayal of ghosts.

Ein Fragment aus dem Leben dreier Freunde

The generally rather easygoing and humorous tale "Ein Fragment aus dem Leben dreier Freunde" was written in late 1816 and first published in the periodical *Der Wintergarten* in 1818. The account was subsequently included in the first volume of *Die Serapionsbrüder* in the succeeding year.

The structure of this tale bears a striking resemblance to the frame of the collection where several people recount stories and anecdotes to each other. It relates the experiences of three young friends who have just arrived in the Prussian capital and who meet in a café in the Berliner Tiergarten. One of them, Alexander, informs of remarkable events in a big house which he has inherited from his spinster aunt. He seriously contends that the residence is haunted by her spirit.

While his aunt was still alive, she was used to reenacting her unfortunate wedding day, which she spent waiting for a bridegroom who never came to his wedding. As a ghost, the young man's aunt seems to be continuing this reenactment faithfully. She puts on her bridal garments and waits for her faithless lover. Her tormented spirit is heard but rarely seen. The second friend, Marzell, relates a spooky nocturnal visit by a demented neighbor, Nettelmann, who attempts to read his personality in a water glass to assure himself that the newcomer constitutes no threat to him. The third friend, Severin, who is sickly, contributes a highly bizarre tale of a type of illumination which he has encountered in a park, set off by an odor of roses and carnations.

This mutual storytelling is interrupted when the three young men's attention is attracted to a very beautiful girl sitting with her family at a nearby table. The girl has just been handed a note and seems to be severely grief-stricken upon reading it. The men speculate about the possible content of the note and then go their separate ways.

Several years later, the friends meet again and it turns out that, after their previous gathering, they have all pursued the mysterious young woman whose name is Pauline. Marzell, by chance gaining access to her house, cultivates her friendship and prepares to declare his love for her when he learns that the note she had been given in the café was not, as he had assumed, from a competitor, but rather a milliner's message that her new hat from Paris had been ruined. Marzell, who sees it both as a personal duty and a passion to console women abandoned by their lovers, is so perplexed and dismayed by this surprising information that he runs off to join the army.

Another of the three friends, Severin, on learning where the young woman lives, visits the area in the hope of seeing her, and indeed appears to detect her standing at an upper window. He sends her a note declaring his love, elaborating on his remarkable floral vision, and asking her to stand at the window at a certain time. At the appointed time her father appears instead, mocking Severin, at which point the latter understands his folly and, like his friend, joins the army. The third friend, Alexander, on the other hand, has found that the haunting of his house decreased when he fell in love with a neighbor girl, whom he eventually married. As we learn at the end of the story, this is none other than the beautiful Pauline.

The author relates the tale in a deliberately light vein. The three young men are fashionably nonchalant and cavalier about their stories. Alexander, who is known as a skeptic, narrates the account half-jokingly, and the reader would have suspected deception if the young man had not turned pale upon discovering that Severin believes the story. This changes the atmosphere drastically. The pronounced rationalist Alexander is shocked. The depicted haunting reveals itself in the sound of footsteps, groans, sighs, coughing, and the sound of someone opening a cabinet and taking medicine (as it later turns out, for digestive problems); afterwards, a white figure appears by the wall. The aunt's dog, still present in her old home, is heard whimpering and nervously scratching at the door.

Alexander, at first paralyzed by terror at the haunting, faints and later concludes that he has had a nightmare, particularly considering the fact that he is unable to find a medicine cabinet in the room. He reconsiders this position, however, when the old housekeeper Anne, uncovers a concealed medicine cabinet and confirms the haunting. She only senses this supernatural manifestation solely on the anniversary of the wedding that never took place, and not night after night, as Alexander experiences it. She also hears the sounds of the whole wedding preparation and some of the aunt's comments.

Marzell, although not rejecting the notion of spiritual manifestations, makes the familiar objection of materialistic banality in regard to the medicine cabinet detail. Severin's reaction is thoughtful; banal details he explains, very often appear in dreams, where they seem to represent nature's irony of its present imperfect state. (*Werke* 6:129) Therefore the disincarnate psyche, as a "geistiges Prinzip" may display a similar irony in pondering its former corporeality. It is certainly valid to point out that Severin is later ridiculed as an absurd dreamer, but the author's derision falls on dreamer and rationalist alike, and too much concern has gone into his comment for the reader to dismiss it too hastily. With regards to the apparition itself, lacking any evidence that a hallucination is somehow involved, it is natural to feel compelled to embrace it as a reality within the story.

From the point of view of Todorov's theory, the tale fits the category of a pure fantastic tale where the hesitation of the reader remains throughout the story. Since the existence of the aunt's ghost is never disproved, the end of the story offers no direct resolution to the problem of what is actually taking place. It could even be argued that the existence of the ghost appears to be so irrefutable that there is no real reason for hesitation on the part of the reader. The story could then be considered marvelous rather than fantastic. Still, the narrative lacks many of the traditional elements of a marvelous tale. As opposed to a typical fairy tale for instance, the supernatural component is restricted to one element in the story, albeit a very important one. It is also interesting to note that the story fits well into Todorov's suggestion that the fantastic virtually by definition is connected with repressed sexuality and passion.

As in some other of Hoffmann's stories, such as "Das Majorat," this ghost story serves as a background for a tale of such exalted passion, though not necessarily immediately associated with it. In the café, the three young men feel the simultaneous impact of obsession with Pauline and intoxication (the punch). Words appear to assume strange and improper connotations, and the barren landscape is magically enhanced. Marzell and Severin, in their unavailing courtship, represent, each in his way, the mechanics of exaltation. They embody it, no doubt, in an unflattering way. The narrative can be interpreted as a rationalistic comedy in which the idiocy of pure infatuation (intense but temporary), is juxtaposed with real, adult love. Marzell considers the moment when he first saw Pauline as the holiest of his life. He claims that the memory of it is like a flaming arrow piercing his vitals. Upon seeing her again, he becomes mute and fears that he will fall down on the spot. Pauline and her father, it later turns out, have noticed this very exalted state. Pauline regards it as a result of his war experiences, whereas the father simply attributes it to alcohol. Marzell eventually discovers that he does not really love Pauline. The author is at his most skeptical about the nature of passion here, but the nature of his skepticism needs to be correctly understood. It is highly unlikely that one can talk about pure infatuation or "puppy love" in this case. It is not the intensity of the passion as such that is questioned, but rather its correspondence to reality. It is presented as an entirely subjective process fueled by the unattainableness of the object and indifferent to the real nature of that same object. The author seems to regard psychosis as a conceivable result when the unfulfilled (and probably unfulfillable) longing reaches a peak of frustration, or when, as in this particular case, its subjective character is revealed. The reader is reminded of this risk by the appearance of the deranged man called Nettelmann, with whom Marzell is at one point confused. Overtly, the tale contrasts real love with infatuation or self-centered erotic passion. A covert meaning could possibly be that all love is actually self-centered erotic passion.

Severin, the second of the suitors, display traits very similar to those revealed by Marzell. They thus both represent, in the form of a light caricature, the various patterns of exaltation. Marzell, the extrovert, shows his fixation in hypomanic behavior, approaching mad hysteria, whereas Severin is preoccupied with inner visions.

The third and ultimately successful suitor, Alexander, disregarding his ghost-seeing proclivity, lacks the neurotic oddities that afflict his two companions. Therefore, his love-relationship can be considered normal in contrast to theirs, something which the essentially comic nature of the story requires. Even though Alexander sometimes loses himself in reveries of passionate love, he carries out his courtship with calculated deliberateness. Alexander, who once perceived something uncanny about brides, now considers matrimony to be his "Lebensglück."

It is interesting to note how closely the haunting appears to be connected with his relation to and experience of love. The haunting was at its worst after the encounter in the Berliner Tiergarten. It later decreases when the love affair blossoms. It is therefore easy to conclude that the haunting is only imagined by Alexander as a result of his erotic frustrations. That is, however, hardly Hoffmann's intent. Pauline's father, for instance, becomes pensive on hearing the story of the haunting and accepts its reality while at the same time attacking what he perceives as the narrow rationalism of the Enlightenment. The atmosphere of mystery thus remains.

"Ein Fragment aus dem Leben dreier Freunde" is the first of Hoffmann's tales to contrast the protagonist's panic over the urge to marry with a friend's comparable experience, and it is also the first of three such narratives, the other two being "Meister Martin der Küfner" and "Die Brautwahl," which depict an impatient competition among three suitors for the same attractive young woman. The author's adaptations of this type of tale also include stories in which only two confidants are captivated by the same lady, such as "Der Kampf der Sänger," "Der Elementargeist" and "Meister Floh."

Like Theodor in the brief narrative "Das öde Haus," the protagonist in "Ein Fragment aus dem Leben dreier Freunde" blames his own love crisis on the insanity of a spurned old maid, who is, in this case of course, his aunt. Alexander's tale about his old affluent relative's apparition is related as an almost jesting rationalization of the urge to marry that he has experienced since coming into an inheritance. He decides to settle in Berlin, initially to enjoy bachelor life in the comfort of the aunt's spacious house, and then, as a happily married man, after having fallen in love with Pauline Asling and having absolved the civil duty which called him away from the capital and his attempts to find the woman of his dreams. The apprehension that seizes most of the author's bachelors does not cause Alexander to panic, or at least his half-ironic joking about his aunt's spirit makes it possible for him to conquer his fears. It could be noted that his name recalls Alexander the great, and much more recently, Alexander the First of Russia, one of the victors in the struggle against Napoleon. The protagonist of this tale in fact emerges as the first fortunate spouse among the central character's of Hoffmann's stories, as later, under comparable circumstances, Moritz in "Der unheimliche Gast" becomes the first joyous expectant father among the author's amorous young men.

The wedding which concludes the story is held in the haunted house on the portentous anniversary, the time of maximum haunting. A gentle sigh is heard and all present are permeated by an electric warmth. Since then, no haunting has ever been observed in the house.

If we accept the idea that the ghost is indeed the disincarnate and sentient spirit of the aunt, no explanation is needed as to why her appearances decline as she finds vicarious fulfillment in her nephew's love affair. One could also argue, however, that the ghost represents Eros and anti-Eros at the same time; i.e., erotic desire combined with dejected chastity.

The lighthearted nature of this story sharply contrasts with most of Hoffmann's supernatural tales, which tend to be much more somber in nature. The fateful atmosphere in a story like "eine Spukgeschichte" is a case in point. It should be noted, as a final observation, that the humor involved in "Ein Fragment aus dem Leben dreier Freunde" is not intended to negate the validity of accepting at least the possibility of the existence of ghosts. Also in this sense, the narrative is entirely compatible with the Todorovian notion of the fantastic. The story is interesting in part because of its light-hearted almost playful nature, but this should not make the reader forget the clear affinity with Hoffmann's many other supernatural tales, including the somber "Eine Spukgeschichte."

Eine Spukgeschichte

"Eine Spukgeschichte" (also called "Der schwebende Teller") was published in the second volume of *Die Serapionsbrüder* in 1819 after having initially been printed in *Der Freimüthige* earlier the same year. This brief account, with its deliberate creation of hesitation on the part of the reader, also very well suits

Todorov's framework of the pure fantastic. The tale is one of the author's more frightening ghost stories and depicts the destructive influence of the notorious apparition known as the white lady ("die weiße Frau"). The part of the frame which includes the conversation of the members of the Serapion Circle preceding "Eine Spukgeschichte" is important since it sheds light on possible interpretations of the story itself.

The short frame after "Der Kampf der Sänger" and before "Eine Spukgeschichte" is a combination of ironic remarks on psychic forces and literature, mixed with pensive conversation and anecdotal material about magnetism. The incomplete scraps of dialogue and the mildly depreciative comments emphasize the seriousness of the key topics at the same time that they assist the reader in understanding psychic forces. Magnetism once again stands in the forefront, with Cyprian advocating its diagnostic potential and contending that the poets, as the "darlings" of nature, should naturally learn her secrets. (*Werke* 6:69–70) The fascination of magnetism for the *Serapionsbrüder* is apparent in Ottmar's remark that he finds the subject tiresome, but he nonetheless goes on immediately to narrating a tale which deals with magnetic powers. (*Werke* 6:70)

The two anecdotes, Ottmar's and Theodor's, both depict objects that appeared to move autonomously but were brought in motion by the concentration of someone nearby. The psycho-kinetic forces at work here depend on the strength of the will of the individual attempting to move the inanimate objects. These anecdotes, according to Ziegler, directly foreshadow a similar one in "Eine Spukgeschichte." (Ziegler 194) The fact that inanimate objects and individuals obtain the force of the magnetizer's character would appear, as Ziegler also concludes, to have an obvious connection with the concerns presented in the frame at the beginning of the book and with "Der Kampf der Sänger" as well as with the subsequent tales "Eine Spukgeschichte" and "Die Automate." (Ziegler 194) In all those cases, the major female characters of the narrative seem to be under the control of an exceptionally strong will. (Ziegler 194) In contrast to a story like "Nußknacker und Mausekönig," the sources of these psychic forces in "Eine Spukgeschichte" and "Die Automate" are never explained.

As so many of the stories in the collection, "Eine Spukgeschichte" has several purposes, some associated with the frame itself, others with the overall theme, and others with relation to the inner tales. The account serves to display the reality of the spirit world, thereby reinforcing some of the other narratives. A tale such as "Eine Spukgeschichte," which exemplifies the nature of this "Fremden psychischen Prinzips," assists in convincing the members of circle of the *Serapionsbrüder* that it is a genuine peril which they encounter when they expand perception to the edge of consciousness. This particular tale makes such menacing characters appear authentic and hints at the intervention of curious psychic forces into everyday life, as is also the case of Ferdinand and Ludwig in "Die Automate," whom the reader is already familiar with from the earlier story "Der Dichter und Komponist".

Cyprian underscores the proximity of this danger by attributing his own apprehensive frame of mind to these occurrences and confirms the veracity of the tale. He then places it in the context of recent events. (*Werke* 6:73) In order to make the other circle members sense the complete terror which befalls the family, Cyprian spends the first part of the account depicting their personalities in some detail. The colonel is good-tempered and cheerful, his spouse reticent and uncomplicated, the older of the two daughters exceptionally animated as well as pretty. (*Werke* 6:73)

In this amiable and spirited group, there is only one troubling character, the beautiful younger daughter Adelgunde, who appears haunted. (*Werke* 6:74) Her symptoms are clearly identifiable as those of an individual under the sinister influence of a harmful external power. Cyprian has just found out that her illness has been caused by a seemingly childish venture to imitate the ghost of the feared "weiße Frau" at her own birthday party.

In his edition of Hoffmann's works, Hans Joachim Kruse observes that this same apparition appears frequently in ghost stories and always brings sorrow. One source is supposedly a countess, Agnes von Orlaumünde, who murdered her two children. As atonement for this mortal sin, she is forced to appear after her death, in order to warn the Hohenzollerns of impending family difficulties. (Kruse 709) Adelgunde confronts this tragic figure of the white lady as an unexpected result of her birthday celebration, which in part takes place outside the family house. Even though the children have been playing in the forest for some time, they do not notice the approaching darkness. The magical twilight ("magische Dämmerung") seduces them to play at elves and spirits. (*Werke* 6:75) Adelgunde, with a white shawl wrapped around her, stares in terror, because she is the only one who is able to see the white lady. Despite several attempts by her family to dissuade her or even to trick her out of seeing the ghost, the young girl sees the white lady every night at nine o'clock.

The ghost has pushed Adelgunde to the brink of insanity, but when the girl attempts to throw a plate at the spirit, the dished is stopped, then carried by an unseen hand and placed on the table. This supernatural display of power drives the rest of the family to destruction. The mother dies soon after the occurrence, the father falls at the battle of Waterloo under peculiar circumstances, and the older sister loses her mind. The younger daughter herself, however, has been healed by the strange encounter and now cares for her demented sister. The nearness of the menace to the *Serapionsbrüder* is underscored by the allusion to Dr. R, whose arrival for consultation is quickly approaching.

The members of the circle react to Cyprian's account with discernible unease. Ottmar retells its chief components, which makes these occurrences even more authentic to the reader and he applies rational perspective to it with the result that he cannot explain such happenings. To add to their distress, Ottmar notes that he has learned from fellow officers that the last battle of the colonel was curious: "...der Obrist sei beim Angriff plötzlich wie von Furien getrieben ins feindliche Feuer hineingesprengt." (*Werke* 6:80) These "furies," apparently perceived by the officer during Napoleon's final battle, add even greater eeriness to the already somber tale.

The lack of an explanation, combined with the plausibility of the account, strengthen its disturbing impact. Ottmar offers a significant indication of the purpose of these frame reports when he states: "...und das Ganze so ungesucht, so einfach, daß gerade in der Wahrscheinlichkeit, die das Unwahrscheinlichste dadurch erhält, für mich das grauenhafte liegt." (*Werke* 6:80) The occurrences which take place in the lives of people known to the members of the circle are not only more terrifying because they happen to acquaintances, but because they take place in a way and in an environment which is very authentic.

"Eine Spukgeschichte," just as the magnetic anecdotes, portrays control of the will by an outside force. Theodor describes the terror he experiences in relation to these influences, stressing the despairing sense of helplessness: "Es ist das Gefühl der gänzlichen hülflosesten Ohnmacht, das den Geist zermalmen müßte." (*Werke* 6:80) Theodor augments his words with a short anecdote about a childhood memory. The participation of several group members in this conversation leads Lothar to complain that he cannot stand the proliferation of such tales, which stress the attraction and repulsion that the circle, like the characters in the narratives, feel toward psychic forces. (*Werke* 6:79) Just as, at the end of the discussion of Serapion, the demand for relief from threatening subjects becomes apparent. Theodor, as in the first book, takes charge to lead the circle back to a supposedly less troubled reality with the fragment of a story.

"Eine Spukgeschichte" reminds the reader of Roxanne Eminescu's analysis of the fantastic where she stresses the importance of the ultimate malaise which the reader feels after having finished the story and after, in a sense, having lost confidence in the natural world. (Eminescu 213) Not only the young girl in the tale feels the sickness, but so also (on the mental level) does the reader or listener to the tale (something which the succeeding conversation among the *Serapionsbrüder* also strongly underscores). The supernatural elements in another tale, "Der Artushof," are in some ways much more subtle than in "Eine Spukgeschichte" and therefore also substantially more vague, to a point, in fact, that this narrative has occasionally been perceived by some readers to have few supernatural elements.

Der Artushof

"Der Artushof" was written in 1815 and first published in *Urania* in 1817. It became a part of *Die Serapionsbrüder* in 1819. The narrative begins in the famous building with the same name in Danzig, which was used for a long time as a meeting place for merchants and businessmen and as a kind of stock exchange. The protagonist of the story is a young businessman called Traugott who is an assistant in the Artushof to a rich merchant named Elias Roos. Since the former has put much of his own fortune into the business, Roos tolerates his ineptitude and has even arranged a marriage between him and his daughter Christina.

Traugott's eyes wander from his random occupation with business transactions to the murals, especially to one depicting a burgomaster of olden days and a beautiful youth. Involuntarily one day he copies these two figures on the "Aviso" he is supposed to be writing. This sets a series of supernatural events in motion. He sees the figures of the picture before him. Almost immediately thereafter, two visitors to the hall appear. The older of the men mitigates the anger of the senior business partner when he praises Traugott's talents as an artist. The younger visitor (his son) presents a very bleak picture of the life of an artist, stressing its financial insecurity. The older visitor, however, presents himself as an artist and offers to take Traugott as a pupil. The latter leaves his desk in Artushof and renounces the hand of Christina.

Berklinger, the artist, explains that he himself has painted the mural in his early days using himself as a model for the central figure and his son as the page. Later on, the old artist mysteriously presents a blank canvass as his "greatest work." The younger artist eventually is drawn more and more to Berklinger's son and eventually discovers that he is actually the artist's daughter Felizitas. At this point, Berklinger angrily throws the young man out of the house. In accordance with a prophecy, the old artist believes that he will instantly die when his daughter falls in love.

The following day the protagonist discovers that both the old man and his daughter have disappeared. He searches for them with great energy, but finds only the cryptic words: "Gone to Sorrento." He does not find them in Italy, but is impressed by the country itself and the artistic world there. A rumor of an old painter and his daughter reaches his ears. Traugott seeks them out; they are not Berklinger and his daughter, even though the daughter Domina strongly resembles the missing girl. The young artist becomes a friend of the family.

Later, the death of Elias Roos demands Traugott's return to Danzig. There the mystery of Berklinger's disappearance is solved. A town councillor owned a big house near the city which he had named "Sorrento" and there he had hidden the fugitives. What Berklinger had feared the most has happened: His daughter has had a suitor, and her father dies as the prophecy has predicted. She later marries a "Kriminalrat" in Marienwerder, and, as a spouse of this official, has ceased to cast a spell over the protagonist. Traugott concludes his business dealings and returns to Italy and to Domina.

As one enters the peculiar world of the main characters of the "Der Artushof," where the figures in the paintings keep coming out of their frames, the fantastic world appears to be closer than when the elderly spinster of "Fragment aus dem Leber dreier Freunde" went to the medicine cabinet during her haunting. Part of the reason for the heavier stress on supernatural elements lies in the artistic nature of the protagonist Traugott, who is more open to such influences than the bourgeois figures of the preceding story. The main character of "Der Artushof" would have fled as quickly from the establishment in the Grünstraße and Pauline as from the Danzig stock exchange and Christina. The shock value of the fantastic, as Horst Conrad has pointed out, is increased by the fact that the sudden appearance of a man who claims to be Godofreus Berklinger takes place in a center of philistinism, the stock exchange. (Conrad 69).

As is the case in the preceding tale, "Der Artushof" has a substantial amount of local color. Furthermore, the latter story also emerges from the experience of one of the members of the Serapion circle, in this case Cyprian. The position of the tale in the series of accounts of the second night is paradigmatic as well as cautionary: paradigmatic due to Traugott's final insight, and cautionary because of the constant danger of insanity that surrounds the artist, as in the case of Berklinger. The latter's madness has a more crippling effect on his art than Serapion's does on his, since Serapion can still write, whereas Berklinger is no longer able to paint. There is, as Lothar Pikulik has observed, a clear parallel with Rat Krespel in two areas: the protection of a beautiful daughter and in his attempts to use his art as a key to understanding hidden secrets. (Pikulik 84–85) The problem of artistic expression is also a factor in Traugott's realization of Felizitas as an inspiration separate from daily life and this is representative of the author's artists, as Theodor had already demonstrated in "Die Fermate." This similarity of themes, as Vickie Ziegler has noted, ties the first and second sections together; in Theodor's case, life experience makes such a separation necessary; in "Der Artushof," the insight results from an inner vision. (Ziegler 156)

An aspect which has been at least in part neglected is Berklinger's significance in establishing correlations that reach forward and backward. Christa Karoli has observed his affinity with Zacharias Werner in an article on Hoffmann's relations to Werner. His connections with characters such as Serapion and to a lesser extent with Elias Fröbom, as well as with Cardillac, Heinrich von der Ofterdingen and Baron von B. have not received the same attention. Berklinger, it should be noted, is also the first artist in the collection who falls victim to insanity.

The protagonist Traugott is not only a character representative of this particular story but also a more general model. In tales such as "Der Kampf der Sänger" and "Die Brautwahl," young artists who are motivated by attractive women to superb artistic creativity end by abandoning any wish or expectation to live with this person. Traugott understands that motivation in its embodied form (such as in the shape of a woman) is not able to live with the artist in the natural world of daily life. At the end of the story, when Traugott ponders his loss of Felizitas, he realizes that he will always have her, because she is the spirit of creative art which lives in him: "Nein, nein, Felizitas, nie habe ich dich verloren, du bleibst mein immerdar, denn du selbst bist ja die schaffende Kunst, die in mir lebt." (*Werke* 5:195) Traugott understands that it is unnecessary to see women again who have been an original inspiration. Such a woman can only live inside the artist if she is to continue to motivate him.

The character of Godefredus Berklinger, the mysterious painter of an earlier period, is the first of several revenants, such as Torbern in "Die Bergwerke zu Falun," and Meister Leonhard and the Münzjude in "Die Brautwahl." It could be argued that the author's tendency to use this type of figure serves to symbolize both the perils and the absence of barriers in the process of self-realization. The character of Berklinger also alludes to the "old German" motif into the tale. For the author, this period, by which he understood the fifteenth and sixteenth centuries, was a time of exceptional artistic creativity. When Berklinger contends that he is the painter whose work in the Artushof was finished several centuries earlier, he comments on the period: "Überhaupt war es doch...eine herrliche grünende, blühende Künstlerzeit." (Werke 5:179) The author often turned to these artistically fertile periods to motivate his characters and his readers.

This older German age stimulates Traugott to leave the world of Aviso letters and become an artist. The murals in the stock market hall, a mute appearance of art in the midst of a multitude of Philistines, offer a tableau at the beginning of the story which symbolizes the background of the narrative. Traugott is, as mentioned, an associate and the future son-in-law of Elis Roos. There is no understanding for art among Roos and his associates. Even the businessmen who can see the protagonist's talents are otherwise limited in their vision. They consider the artist a type of maniac, or art as a socially acceptable way of relaxation from business activities. The, in many ways, admirable daughter of Elis Roos, Christina, shares these limitations. She could be considered a spiritual cousin of Veronika Paulmann in "Der goldene Topf ". In his essay "Künstlerliebe und Philistertum im Werk E.T.A. Hoffmanns," Karl Ludwig Schneider concludes that the reason why Christina and similar characters are such excellent cooks and such practical women is to stress their difference from the angelic female who inspires art, and who appears to have shed all earthly preoccupations.[1]

In such a cultural wasteland, the wall paintings are the only manifestation of art for the protagonist, and particularly for the beautiful youth in rich clothes. These figures draw Traugott to the edges of the artistic world, they make him sketch their portrait, and they subsequently address him in the middle of the exchange. The similarity of the purpose of the murals in "Der Artushof" with the painting in "Die Fermate" shows yet another parallel between the stories. In the latter tale, the picture motivated the disclosure of an inner narrative. In "Der Artushof," the picture serves the purpose of inspiring the rest of the account. But it is a tale which has not yet been told; instead the mural serves as a motivation for what is to come.

Traugott is the first fictional character in the collection to represent the figure of the ambitious young artist, an often reappearing character in the tales included in *Die Serapionsbrüder*. Of these characters, Traugott and Antonio in "Signor Formica" have the most problems in liberating themselves from the confines of the Philistine world.

The protagonist of "Der Artushof" eventually understands that he does not belong in the stock market where he is more and more distracted by the murals. The drawing of the man and a beautiful young boy in the mural, his first attempt at drawing, makes him remember that, even when he was a boy, these two figures attracted his attention through a power which appears almost magical:

...und er erinnerte sich recht gut, daß schon damals jene Figuren seltsam auf ihn wirkten, und er einst in der Abenddämmerung wie von einer unwiderstehlichen Gewalt von Knabenspiele fort in den Artushof gelockte, wo er sich emsig bemühte, das Bild abzuzeichnen. (*Werke* 5:176)

The allusion to the childhood experience serves two purposes: first of all, it implies that Traugott is predestined to become an artist. The mention of the event in the protagonist's childhood also adds an element of the irrational, since children are rarely capable of formulating an analytical response in the manner of an adult. This emotional feature manifests itself in the above depiction, in which the important encounter takes place in the evening, when an irrepressible power attracts the young boy. Childhood functions in this passage as a symbol of the enigmatic forces involved in the pursuit of art and self-knowledge.

Despite the less than hospitable milieu in which he has to work, the protagonist attains the fundamental Serapionic quality of the artist, even before the old artist agrees to giving him lessons: "...so vermag er, was sein inneres Auge geschaut, festzubannen, indem er es sinnlich darstellt." (Werke 5:175) Traugott has two objectives: one is to learn from the old artist, and the other is to find Felizitas. Her disguise is a symbol of her unapproachability and foreshadows Traugott's destiny, as the author indicates at the beginning of Traugott's search for himself. (Werke 5:176) The protagonist's infatuation with Felizitas emerges when he sees the portrait and slowly brings the painting of a beautiful woman and the youth in close proximity. The old artist's furious reaction to his pupil when the latter falls at the girl's feet is essential for the protection of Traugott's artistic identity. Berklinger states that Traugott's behavior will kill him and he pulls a knife. (Werke 5:185) Nevertheless it could be said that it is from Traugott's own death as an artist that his teacher protects him. As soon as the protagonist has discovered the real identity of the old artist's daughter, the latter is forced to leave, because he stands under a curse. Berklinger's departure also symbolizes, however, the impossibility of combining artistic motivation and ordinary everyday life. Like his teacher, the protagonist, too, stands under a curse: if he wins Berklinger's daughter, he will die as an artist.

Other parallels between Berklinger and his pupil can be found, particularly in regard to the Artushof. The old artist tells the protagonist about his early days as an artist, describing the period in which he painted the figures in the hall. At that time, King Arthur appeared to him, exhorting him to attain perfection. Through Berklinger's image, Traugott realizes the nature of his vocation. In a function comparable to that of King Arthur, the old artist appears to the protagonist. As is the case of many artistic characters in the collection, there are misgivings regarding Berklinger's sanity. When the old man explains to Traugott who he is, the latter wonders if the person is insane. Berklinger's proud display of a blank canvass, which he says portrays paradise regained, reinforces this impression. The old artist glides into a state in which his comments become less and less comprehensible. His dream world is comparable to that of Serapion and it reinforces the "unreal" quality of his character.

Separated from the old artist's lessons and the captivating company of his daughter, he searches for them to no avail. He internalizes Felizitas more and more and no longer regards her as a distinct person, but portrays her face when he sees women. The strong desire to find her has transformed itself into a spiritualized yearning.

Even from the start, Felizitas has not appeared to be a normal character of everyday life. On the contrary, she seems to be a figure created from the artistic imagination and also seems to come from another time, suddenly appearing in contemporary reality in direct connection with the protagonist's sketch work on the old picture for which she has been a model. In a sense, it could be argued that she appears to be as supernatural as the original characters who have left the painting before the protagonist's very eyes.

Traugott's physical bonds with Felizitas break when he comes back to Danzig to settle some final financial questions. At this point, the protagonist understands that he already has the only Felizitas that he requires. As Pikulik has underscored, Traugott does not need fulfilled love, which presupposes the possession of the beloved one, but rather the unfulfilled love which presupposes a distance to the adored person. The resulting longing is a fundamental precondition for artistic creativity. (Pikulik 87) This realization makes it possible for him to combine the necessities of art with his emotional needs as he prepares for his marriage to Dorina.

The subtle use of supernatural elements in "Der Artushof" makes it a somewhat problematic story from the point of view of a Todorovian analysis. But one trait is clear throughout the story. The reader is never informed about whether the two perceived ghosts are a product of his or her (and the protagonist's) imagination or genuine individuals. This makes "Der Artushof" a classic story within the framework of Todorov's definition of the fantastic. The supernatural features of another tale in *Die Serapionsbrüder*, "Die Automate," are much more "intrusive" and indeed puzzling to the reader.

Die Automate

The brief story "Die Automate" was written in January of 1814 and thus belongs to the earliest of the tales later included in *Die Serapionsbrüder*. A part of the story was published in *Allgemeine Musikalische Zeitung* in February of the same year.

In the fall of 1813, Hoffmann had seen the automatons of J. G. and Friedrich Kaufmann in Dresden and was clearly impressed by these machines. Approximately at the same time, he had read for a second time a description in Johann Wiegleb's *Die natürliche Magie* of one of Wolfgang von Kempelen's automatons which had the shape of a chess-player. One editor of Hoffmann's works, Carl Georg von Maasen, concludes that this latter figure was an important inspiration for the story "Die Automate." (Maasen: 8:323) A confirmation of Hoffmann's interest in automatons can be found in a diary note dated as early as October 2, 1803: "den ganzen Abend läppischer Weise in Wieglebs 'Magie' gelesen und mir vorgenommen einmal wenn die gute Zeit da seyn wird zu Nutz und Frommen aller verständigen die ich bey mir sehe ein Automat anzufertigen."

(*Tagebücher* 53) This fascination was to lead to "die Automate" a decade later. The reading of Heinrich von Kleist's essay "Über das Marionettentheater" which included a discussion of the mechanics of dolls was another inspiration for the author's interest in the subject matter, something which is at least indirectly implied in a letter to Julius Hitzig on July 1, 1812. (*Briefwechsel* 1:339)

The opening scene of "Die Automate" takes place in the present time in a realistic situation. A new, talking automat has turned up in the city, causing considerable investigation and speculation, due to its impressive mechanical skills as well as its manifest intellectual sophistication. Although the tale initially has something of the carnival about it in its depiction of the automatic talking Turk, the narrative is essentially another variation on the theme of mysterious powers that dramatically enter into normal daily life. The author's fascination with these remarkable machines is evident in his portrayal of the Turk, who appears to be dead and alive simultaneously (the use of the word "Lebendtot" also confirms this), entirely mechanical, yet seemingly able to answer every question posed.

The ensuing evaluation of the Turk's abilities is a curious combination of technical definitions, hypothesis and amazement. Hoffmann's fascination with such figures lay in part, as Otto Nipperdey claims in his study "*Wahnsinnsfiguren bei E.T.A. Hoffmann,*" in the combination of technical aspects which could be explained and other qualities which could not. But in the inexplicable in the behavior of the mechanical Turk, such as his knowledge of Ferdinand's secret, lies the degree of evil that lurked for the author in every psychic force which could not be explained. The dispiriting and terrifying impact of automatic characters is rooted in their ability to ruin the soul. Such creatures, with at least seemingly lifeless, emptily staring eyes, can foreshadow the fate of an individual who falls under their power, as the related narrative "Der Sandmann" demonstrates.

There are direct references in the text itself to the devilish "mechanical evil" which the automaton can, in the author's view, represent. The following comment from one of the main characters, a young man called Ludwig, is telling in this regard: "Mir sind alle solche Figuren, die dem Menschen nicht sowohl nachgebildet, als das Menschliche nachäffen, diese wahren Standbilder eines lebebendigen Totes oder eines toten Lebens, im höchsten Grade zuwieder." (*Werke* 6:84)

Sometimes, as has also been suggested by Silvio Vietta, the automaton appears to work as the magnetizer putting the subject in touch with his innermost spirit, which is otherwise beyond reach. Ludwig wonders if, in responding to questions, this being can acquire a psychic influence over anyone who poses a question. He suggests that due to this rapport, the automaton evokes an ecstasy in which everything one sees with the eyes of the soul is brightly illuminated. (Werke 6:99–100) Even though Ludwig attempts to minimize the effect of the Turk by comparing it unfavorably to the nutcracker he had as a child, the potential of the machine without any doubt troubles him.

It is through psychic bonds that the automaton acquires information which only one other creature has, as in Ferdinand's case the mysterious singer. Just as in a dream, the person is able to understand matters otherwise concealed, and the automaton is capable of benefitting from this information. Even though this state of affairs connects the tale with the previous one as well as with the frame discussions, its linkage of the automaton with the powers of the magnetizer gives an indication of why the author was both frightened by and captivated by such machines. Mechanical music-making machines also belong in the realm of the automaton and are also connected with the magnetizer. When Ludwig and Ferdinand visit Professor X, the latter demonstrates the human automatons playing musical instruments. (*Werke* 6:101–102) Ludwig explains their effects on him with phrases similar to those used for the Turk. (*Werke* 6:104)

But although the same protagonist condemns the aspirations of technicians to reproduce or supplant the human voice, he does not reject "die höhere musikalische Mechanik." (*Werke* 6:105) Such efforts are praised by the two friends since they assist in revealing the secrets of nature and the music of the spheres. Because Ferdinand does not completely comprehend his friend's expectations of these undertakings, the latter utilizes material from Gotthilf Heinrich Schubert's *Ansichten der Nachtseite der Naturwissenschaft* which he quotes extensively. This section of Schubert's work addresses the situation of man in the first Golden Age, when he was still in harmony with nature. At that time, nature surrounded man with sacred music, which spoke of the mysteries of his unceasing activity: "...verkündigte die Geheimnisse ihres ewigen Treiben." (*Werke* 6:106) Remnants of such lost music can still be found in the music of the spheres, music of the air, and the voice of the devil. The contemporary instrument nearest to this previous perfection is the glass harmonica. (*Werke* 6: 106–107)

There are several reasons which could explain why the author uses this passage in the narrative at this point. By placing Schubert on the side of the higher musical mechanics, he motivates this exploration for new knowledge in the trust that it will reveal concealed harmonies in new levels of perception. Through music, as in a dream under magnetic influence, the spirit can rediscover what lies in its innermost parts and bring it to conscious life:

> Ist es nicht vielmehr das Gemüt, welches sich nur jener psychischen Organe bedient, um das, was in seiner tiefsten Tiefe erklungen, in das rege Leben zu bringen, daß es andern vernehmbar ertönt und die gleichen Anklänge im Innern erweckt, welche dann im harmonischen Widerhall dem Geist das wundervolle Reich erschließen. (*Werke* 6:104)

Such a state makes it conceivable to convey this experience to others. Other remarks concerning the spirit, such as in "Der Kampf der Sänger," make its significance evident. Wolfram's powerful and pure inner spirits attune him to the original harmonies of nature, whereas Heinrich's connections with the devil open his soul to terrible secrets and block him from more constructive comprehension.

Such earlier harmony is, as mentioned, to be found in the glass harmonica. After having lauded the *Glockenharmonika*, Ludwig and Ferdinand hear a mysterious song in a garden close to the city. It is the same aria which Ferdinand has heard earlier and which has radically transformed his inner experience. The author depicts the event in this way: "ein seltsamer Klang durch die Luft, der im stärkern Anschwellen dem Ton einer Harmonika ähnlich wurde." (*Werke* 6:108) The similarity of the girl's voice explains the unique effect which she has on Ferdinand. Silvio Vietta regards her song as sounds functioning as a reminiscence of the original harmonious state of nature. (Vietta 30)

The sublime beauty of the girl's voice, which symbolizes such original harmony, appears to be attainable only in the company of Professor X, who presumably represents concealed knowledge and menacing danger on the one hand, and celestial transfiguration on the other. The precarious potential she presents is corroborated through Theodor's frame allusion to Ferdinand's "somnabulen Liebschaft." (*Werke* 6:112) When the professor demonstrates his musical machines to the two friends, his voice has a dissonant and unpleasant quality, his mouth has a sarcastic expression, and his small eyes blink in a penetrating way. (*Werke* 6:101) Even so when Ludwig and Ferdinand encounter the professor again in the garden with the girl, he appears to show an entirely different side. His repulsive ironic expression is gone and in its place they discover a profound and somewhat despondent seriousness as he stares at the sky, as if he has been transformed and is seeing into the world beyond. As the two friends find out more about Professor X, they realize that musical machines are only a hobby and that his real interests lie in penetrating the secrets of the natural sciences. (*Werke* 6:110) The professor and his female companion represent, on another level, the promise and peril of increasing perception.

As there are no definite answers to the questions raised in the tale, questions symbolized by the figure of the talking Turk, it must remain a fragment. But it is therefore not necessarily, as Ziegler has also observed, a contradictory narrative with vague plot levels. (Ziegler 201) Ferdinand's love story forms an integral part of the author's basic thematic complex addressing the dilemmas of artistic perception and inspiration. Pikulik points out the connection between the artist Traugott in "Der Artushof"and Ferdinand in the theme of the inspirational love of the artist, which can never be possessed. (Pikulik 121–22)

It is unquestionably true that the professor in "Die Automate" is a contradictory character, but the reasons for these inner contradictions lie in the ambivalent nature of the author's belief in concealed knowledge. Such inner connections in the story become evident when one approaches its themes in comparison with the discussion on magnetism, the inexplicable occurrences in "Eine Spukgeschichte," and the contesting characters of the sound artist and the doomed artist in "Der Kampf der Sänger."

The question of perception and comprehension which engages Ludwig at the end of the story hints at the dangerous predicament in which those who test the limits of the psyche find themselves. Ludwig asks himself whether these occurrences could be an effect of the conflict between various psychic relations among a few people, in situations in which outside independent happenings play a part as well, but are included in such a way that they came solely from within himself. (*Werke* 6:112) This probability, that the inner mind misinterprets specific occurrences, is evident, for instance, at the end of "Eine Spukgeschichte," when the narrator refers to the possibility that Adelgunde's delusion might have influenced her family. Stories such as "Die Bergwerke zu Falun," "Der unheimliche Gast," "Der Zusammenhang der Dinge," "Doge and Dogaressa," and "Fräulein von Scuderi" all include illustrative instances of characters whose souls are impacted by mysterious powers and who at times misinterpret these messages, and as a result brings about agony and devastation.

The mysterious forces also demonstrate their fantastic impact in dreams and this too is directly addressed in the story and not only in relation to the enigmatic automaton. The amazing realization of a Traumbild of a woman which Ferdinand has already perceived as a child is a case in point. The young woman later appears before him in real life. This phenomenon is, as in some other tales by Hoffmann, closely connected with the emotion of love. When someone is in love the clear borderline between reality and imagination becomes much more vague. Truth and fiction no longer are reliable criteria for the perceptive faculties. In his study on "Die Automate," Gerhard Weinholz suggests that the author's love for Julia Marc is a direct inspiration for the tremendous impact of love on Ferdinand in this narrative.[2]

After the end of the tale, Ottmar shows irritation because the narrative has not tied up all loose ends. Theodor motivates his method of presenting the account with a defense of fragments which lead into a short comment on fantasy, story-telling and history. He fiercely attacks tales which do not leave room for the reader's imagination, and further expresses his opinion that a story without loose ends is distasteful to him, just because the reader has no questions left to further entice his natural curiosity, since the "historic broom" has swept the stage clean. (*Werke* 6:113)

The historic broom ("der historische Besen") could possibly be considered a metaphor for the rationalistic approach to history, which aspired to view it as a logical and inevitable sequence of events. Because such a method avoids speculation, it does not allow for investigations at the fringes of perception or for expansion of the understanding of what goes on behind the scenes. One scholar, Bernard Casper, regards perception as the most essential component in Hoffmann's view of history, without which the occurrence would lack meaning or cannot even be said to have taken place at all.[3]

"Die Automate" is a fine illustration of Todorov's concept of the "pure" fantastic. The fantastic elements in the account are never explained or in any way rationalized by Hoffmann. The author in fact chooses to leave the whole story in a fragmentary form thereby deliberately reinforcing the reader's hesitation and amazement when confronting the text. Reality and components of the imaginative grotesque are cleverly combined in part simply to mystify the reader, and possibly, as Weinholz has proposed, to confront him or her with the nature of that which is undeniably real in our lives. (Weinholz 53)

The presentation of ghosts and automatons in Hoffmann's tales exemplify a classical feature of the fantastic as the genre has been approached by scholars such as Todorov and Vax. Such supernatural creatures thus become a natural part of a supernatural atmosphere.

Conclusion

The discussion of the short story collection *Die Serapionsbrüder* presented in this study has demonstrated that the order of the stories has not been arbitrarily arranged, as has been proposed by some literary scholars. The sequence chosen possesses on the contrary an overall aesthetic homogeneity. The frame is therefore essential in the interpretation of the collection as a whole, as it normally addresses the content of the included inner tales in one way or another.

The inner stories also, however, frequently relate directly to one other. An example from the very beginning of the collection is the juxtaposition of Serapion and Krespel, which offers the reader significant insight to the understanding of both characters. The placement of the Serapion tale at the outset of the work balances the appearance of Serapion's real-life counterpart, Zacharias Werner, near the end of the collection, and demonstrates the significance of the relationship between creativity and insanity that tends to overshadow other themes in at least some of the earlier stories in the collection.

Madness is another theme of great significance in the account immediately following the depiction of Serapion in the first book of the collection, namely the complex and sometimes deliberately contradictory narrative "Rat Krespel." Since this story leaves the reader to interpret the nature of the main character's sanity/insanity, this tale adds a new aspect to the topic of madness. Hesitation on the part of the reader with regards to what actually takes place in "Rat Krespel" is rather typical of one common tendency in Hoffmann's works. This also makes the tale very suitable to a Todorovian theoretical approach since Todorov has made hesitation a cornerstone of the definition of fantastic literature. A later account in *Die Serapionsbrüder*, "Der Baron von B.," could be considered a companion piece to "Rat Krespel" since it depicts the life of a supposedly mad musician. The description of the eccentric Baron is, however, not quite as complex and contradictory as the presentation of the fascinating Krespel, one of Hoffmann's most colorful characters .

The theme of insanity, (often related to the dark side of consciousness), which reveals itself solely on the individual level in the first narratives, later moves into territory that goes well beyond this level in later stories in the collection. After the author has introduced the realm of the supernatural in a less than somber fashion in the story "Ein Fragment aus dem Leben dreier Freunde," the same fantastic world enters into everyday life as a source of inspiration in the revenant Godefredus Berklinger in the narrative "Der Artushof" and as a devastating menace to sanity in the account "Die Bergwerke zu Falun." In the latter tale mysterious powers take hold of an individual and drive him to self-destruction thereby starting to expose their most threatening facets. Later in the collection, revenants from a distant past reappear, for example, in the long tale "Die Brautwahl" where competing supernatural forces of good and evil engage in a battle on a supernatural level.

The supernatural realm that figures already so conspicuously in some of the first tales also is a core topic of the discussions in the frame. In this context, a long discussion of magnetism which includes a substantial amount of specific details, offers scientific interpretations of mysterious powers (the talking Turk in "Die Automate," is one example) which appear to have a hypnotic impact on some inner-story characters. Other examples are the mysterious figures in the same story as well as the ghost in the rather frightening narrative "Eine Spukgeschichte" (also called "Der schwebende Teller"). A much more light-hearted look at the phenomenon of ghosts is presented in the more humorous tale "Fragment aus dem Leben dreier Freunde." But not only frightening or more entertaining ghosts are aspects of supernatural phenomena in Hoffmann's production. The devil himself also appears in the author's fiction.

The frame in the third book of *Die Serapionsbrüder* introduces an amusing discussion of the nature of the devil. The anecdote "Nachricht aus dem Leben eines bekannten Mannes" also demonstrates enough of Satan's darker side to add troubling notes. Demonic characters (who are therefore not necessarily direct manifestations of the devil himself) often emerge as significant actors in some of the stories of the collection. The devilish powers of the deceitful Count S with his truly horrifying supernatural powers in "Der unheimliche Gast" is an excellent case in point.

It should be noted, however, that the victims of the magnetic forces of evil sometimes are even more important in the author's stories than the demonic characters themselves. A pertinent example is the tormented artist Cardillac in "Das Fräulein von Scuderi" who is driven to murder by evil possession. Another unfortunate victim of the actions of such malevolent powers is the protagonist in the rather long narrative "Die Bergwerke zu Falun," Elis Fröbom, already mentioned above. A totally different type of subjugation under devilish influences is apparent in the short account "Spielerglück" where the main character faces the destructive power of the "Gambler's Devil." In sharp contrast to this kind of evil impact in an everyday setting, a particularly bizarre example of demonic possession is to be found in the rather gruesome narrative "Vampirismus," where topics of vampirism and outright cannibalism are combined; elements that in Todorov's terminology typify the concept of "themes of the other."

Hoffmann's fiction offers many different examples of the fantastic which can be approached with Todorov's theoretical method. The following table attempts to summarize the results of my implementation of Todorov's method on *Die Serapionsbrüder*:

Table 1: Todorovian Classification of Stories

Uncanny		
• Rat Krespel	• Der Baron von B.	• Spielerglück
Fantastic/Uncanny		
• Das Fräulein von Scuderi		
Pure Fantastic		
• Vampirismus	• Der unheimliche Gast	• Eine Spukgeschichte
• Der Artushof	• Die Automate	• Die Bergwerke zu Falun
• Ein Fragment aus dem Leben dreier Freunde		
Fantastic/Marvelous		
• Nachricht aus dem Leben eines bekannten Mannes		
• Die Brautwahl		

As this table clearly demonstrates, Hoffmann's literary production, especially as it is exemplified in *Die Serapionsbrüder*, fits quite nicely into Todorov's concept of the pure fantastic in the majority of cases. The emphasis on the reader's sustained hesitation throughout a story is typical of a Hoffmann story whenever the author approaches fantastic themes. Occasionally, however, he chooses to give either a natural or supernatural explanation to the events which take place in one of his tales. In several cases (for instance in the case of "Nachricht aus dem Leben eines bekannten Mannes") Hoffmann abandons the idea of making the reader hesitate, and simply makes a fantastic story completely "marvelous" (as Todorov defines the word) in a world where the supernatural ultimately is accepted as being real, since an entirely supernatural explanation has been chosen for supernatural events. But such an approach appears to be rare in the author's production. It is interesting to note that Hoffmann uses the opposite, or natural explanation, for a fantastic event only once (in the case of "Das Fräulein von Scuderi") in the whole collection. It seems reasonable to assume that this avoidance of natural explanations would support the conclusion that the author is not primarily interested in dispelling the reader's amazement and hesitation when confronting the fantastic elements of a narrative. On the contrary, he often intends to promote the reader's doubt about the nature of the reality presented in a story and he wishes to retain this hesitation to the very end. This also tends to underscore the validity of the argument that Hoffmann was not principally (if at all) aiming to utilize fantastic elements as features purely designed to reflect the state of mind of the characters involved in a story.

The nature and use of the fantastic in Hoffmann's production as this study has approached these issues from both a theoretical and practical point of view would thus support the conclusion that purely psychological interpretations of the author's inclusion of supernatural elements must be made with great caution. One finds a special case in the "uncanny" stories such as "Rat Krespel" where the fantastic becomes very much a matter of personal interpretation, and where all elements of the tale also can be understood on a purely rational level. A close examination of Hoffmann's choice of the fantastic as a vehicle for various ideas in his fiction shows that his works are too multifaceted to strictly fit into one limited and rigid pattern of explanations. The author's methods with regards to the presentation of the fantastic elements in his works reflect the use of such features both as a literary device (employed with the objective of both stunning and entertaining his readers) as well as the promotion of a belief system emphasizing the importance of the irrational or at the very least a challenge to the reader to contemplate the character of our human existence. In the latter case the issue is not necessarily whether creatures such as ghosts and vampires really exist, but the objective rather appears to be to convey colorful and often frightening images of a menacing and irrational world with the purpose of inspiring reflection about the true nature of reality. Many of Hoffmann's tales consequently become "dark mirrors" of an existence which cannot always be explained using rational logic. In this sense, the author is very much a part of the romantic tradition with its interest in the irrational aspects of life.

Even though the fantastic nature of so much of this writer's œuvre gives his production an artistic unity, one must remember that his use of such components may serve very different functions on different occasions. This study has aspired to demonstrate that Todorov's theoretical system can assist in categorizing Hoffmann's works and systematize his short fiction in a logical way which could hopefully be helpful to any future scholarship dealing with *Die Serapionsbrüder.*

Completed only shortly before the author's death in 1822, the collection is of particular significance for scholarly research on this writer, since it is, in various ways, his most thorough and elaborate literary treatment of a great variety of themes; combining his views on several of the major themes of his production with some of his most interesting short stories in an arrangement and setting that appeared important to him. Future research on the collection should pay further attention to the many fantastic elements which constitute such a central part of the collection's content.

Notes

Chapter One

1 E.T.A. Hoffmann, "Les écarts d'un homme à imagination." *Biblioteque Universelle de Genève* 37 (1828):330.

2 Allienne Rimer Becker, *"The Fantastic in the Fiction of Hoffmann and Hawthorne"* Diss. (Philadelphia: Pennsylvania State University) 29.

3 Pierre-Georges Castex, *Le Conte fantastique en France de Nodier a Maupassant.* (Paris: Coti, 1962) 35.

4 Marcel Schneider, *La littérature fantastique en France* (Paris: Fayard, 1964) 163.

5 Tzvetan Todorov, *Introduction à la littérature fantastique* (Paris: Éditions du Seuil, 1970) 168–69.

6 Roger Caillois, *Anthologie du fantastique* (Paris: Gallimard, 1966) I, 8.

7 Roger Caillois, *Images, Images...* (Paris: José Corti, 1966) 26.

8 Louis Vax, *Séduction de l'étrange* (Paris: Presses Universitaires de France, 1965) 308.

9 Claude Roy, "Psychologie de fantastique," *Les Temps modernes*, (1960): 166–8, 1416.

10 Georges Geo Jacquemin, "Über das Phantastische in Literatur," *Phaicon* 2, ed. Rein Zondergeld (Frankfurt: Insel, 1975): 37.

11 Roxanne Eminescu, "Le fantastique," *Travaux de linguistique et de littérature* 11 (1973): 213.

12 Jacques Finné, *La littérature fantastique*, (Bruxelles: Université de Bruxelles, 1980) 15

13 Stanislaw Lem, "Todorov's Fantastic Theory of Literature: Suggestions on how to define and analyze fantastic fiction," *Science Fiction Studies* 1 (1974): 227.

14 W. Ostrowski, "The Fantastic and the Realistic in Literature: Suggestions on how to define and analyze fantastic fiction," *Zagadnienia rodzajow literackich* 9 (1966): 57.

15 Eric S. Rabkin, The Fantastic in Literature (Princeton: Princeton University Press, 1976) 41.

16 Gary K. Wolfe, "Symbolic Fantasy," *Genre* 8 (1975): 194.

17 Diana Waggoner, *The Hills of Faraway: A Guide to Fantasy* (New York: Athenaeum, 1978) 9.

18   T. E. Apter, *Fantasy Literature: An Approach to Reality* (Bloomington: Indiana UP, 1982) 19.

19   Rein Zondergeld, "Zwei Versuche der Befreiung," *Phaicon* 2, Ed. Rein Zondergeld. (Frankfurt: Insel, 1975) 68.

20   Winfried Freund, "Von der Aggression zur Angst," *Phaicon* 3, ed. Rein Zondergeld (Frankfurt: Suhrkamp, 1978) 11.

21   Winfried Freund, *ed. Phantastische Geschichten* (Stuttgart: Reclam, 1979) 76.

Chapter Two

1   E.T.A. Hoffmann, *Briefwechsel*, 3 vols. eds. Hans von Müller and Friedrich Schnapp (München: Winkler, 1968): 2:437.

2   E.T.A. Hoffmann, *Poetische Werke, 12 vols.* (Berlin: Walter de Gruyter & Co., 1957) 7: 101

3   Joseph Tetinger, *Le Conte fantastique dans le romantisme francais* (Genève: Sklatine Reprints, 1973, reprint of Paris edition of 1909) 25.

4   E.T.A. Hoffmann, *Tagebücher,* ed. Friedrich Schnapp (München: Winkler, 1971) 398, 472.

5   Johanna C. Sahlin, ed. and trans., *Selected Letters of E.T.A. Hoffmann* (Chicago: U of Chicago P) 322.

6   Diana Stone Peters, "E.T.A. Hoffmann: The Conciliatory Satirist," *Monatshefte* 66 (1974): 72.

7   Peter von Matt, "Die gemalte geliebte," *Germanistisch-Romanistische Monatshefte* 21 (1971): 398.

8   Harvey Hewett-Thayer, *Hoffmann: Author of the Tales* (Princeton: Princeton University Press, 1948) 225.

9   Robert Mühlher, "E.T.A. Hoffmann. Beiträge zu einer Motiv-Interpretation," *Literaturwissenschaftliches Jahrbuch der Goethe-Gesellschaft* 4 (1963): 65.

10   Sigmund Freud, "Das Unheimliche," *Gesammelte Werke* (London: Imago, 1947) XII: 234–35.

11   Johannes Klein, *Geschichte der deutschen Novelle von Goethe bis zur Gegenwart* (Wiesbaden: Steiner, 1960) 127.

12   Günter Hartung, "Anatomie des Sandmanns," *Weimarer Beiträge* 23 (1977): 65.

Chapter Three

1   Hans von Müller, *Gesammelte Aufsätze über E.T.A. Hoffmann* (Hildesheim: Verlag Dr. H.A. Gerstenberg ,1974) 676–77.

2   Eckhart Kleßmann, *E.T.A. Hoffmann oder die Tiefe zwischen Stern und Erde* (Stuttgart: Deutsche Verlags–Anstalt, 1988) 431.

3   Lothar Pikulik, *E.T.A. Hoffmann als Erzähler: ein Kommentar zu den "Serapionsbrüdern"* (Göttingen: Vandenhoeck & Ruprecht, 1987) 14–19.

4   Horst Conrad, *Die literarische Angst: Das Schreckliche in Schauerromantik und Detektivgeschichte* (Düsseldorf: Bertelsmann Universitätsverlag, 1974) 76.

5   Peter von Matt, *Die Augen der Automaten: E.T.A. Hoffmanns Imaginationslehre als Prinzip seiner Erzählkunst* (Tübingen: Max Niemeyer Verlag, 1971) 6.

6   Friedhelm Auhuber, *In einem fernen dunklen Spiegel: E.T.A. Hoffmanns Poetisierung der Medizin* (Opladen: Westdeutscher Verlag, 1986) 120.

7   Gotthilf Heinrich Schubert, *Ansichten von der Nachtseite der Naturwissenschaft* (Darmstadt: 1967[1807]) 302.

8   Franz G. Alexander and Sheldon T. Selesnick, *The History of Psychiatry: An Evaluation of Psychiatric Thought and Practice from Prehistoric Times to the Present* (New York: Columbia UP, 1966) 131–32.

Chapter Four

1   Frank Haase, "Eine Marginalie zu E.T.A. Hoffmanns Novelle 'Rat Krespel,'" *Mitteilungen der E.T.A. Hoffmann-Gesellschaft-Bamberg* 31 (1985): 15–16.

2   James McGlathery, *Mysticism and Sexuality: E.T.A. Hoffmann* (New York/Berne: Peter Lang, 1985) 125.

Chapter Five

1   Hans Toggenburger, *Die späten almanach-Erzählungen E.T.A. Hoffmanns* (Bern/New York: Peter Lang, 1983) 51.

2   Hans Joachim Kruse, ed. *E.T.A. Hoffmann: Gesammelte Werke,* (Berlin-Weimar, Aufbau-Verlag, 1978) 602.

3   Karl Olbrich, "E.T.A. Hoffmann und der deutsche Volksglaube," *E.T.A. Hoffmann,* ed. Helmut Prang, (Darmstadt: Wissenschaftliche Buchgesellschaft, 1976) 73–75.

4   Karl Ochsner, *E.T.A. Hoffmann als Dichter des Unbewußten: Ein Beitrag zur Geistelgeschichte der Romantik* (Leipzig: Huber, 1936) 116.

Chapter Six

1   Richard Alewyn, "Ursprung des Detektivromans," *Probleme und Gestalten* (Frankfurt am Main: Insel Verlag 1974) 353.

Chapter Seven

1   Karl Ludwig Schneider, "Künstlerliebe und Philistertum in Werk E.T.A. Hoffmanns," *Die Deutsche Romantik*, ed. Hans Steffen (Göttingen: Vandenhoek & Ruprecht, 1978) 211.

2   Gerhard Weinholz, *E.T.A. Hoffmanns Erzählung "Die Automate"* (Essen: Verlag die Blaue Eule, 1991) 25.

3   Bernhard Casper, "Der historische Besen oder die Geschichtsauffassung in E.T.A. Hoffmanns *Serapionsbrüdern* und in der katholischen Tübinger Schule," *Romantik in Deutschland, ein interdiziplinäres Symposium*, ed. Richard Brinkmann. (Stuttgart: Metzler Verlag, 1978) 490–501.

Selected Bibliography

Primary Sources

Hoffmann, Ernst Theodor Amadeus. *Briefwechsel.* Ed. Hans von Müller and Friedrich Schnapp. München: Winkler, 1967–69.

_____. *Dichter über ihre Dichtung.* Ed. Friedrich Schnapp. München: Heimeran, 1974.

_____. *Gesammelte Werke.* Ed. Hans Joachim Kruse. Berlin-Weimar: Aufbau-Verlag, 1978.

_____. "Les écarts d'un homme a imagination" *Biblioteque Universelle de Geneve* 37. (1828): 300–33.

_____. *Poetische Werke.* Berlin: Walther de Gruyer & Co., 1957–62.

_____. *Sämtliche Werke.* Ed. Georg von Maasen. München und Leipzig: Georg Müller & Propyläen-Verlag, 1908–28.

_____. *Tagebücher.* Ed. Friedrich Schnapp. München: Winkler, 1971.

Secondary Sources

Alewyn, Richard. "Ursprung des Detektivromans." *Probleme und Gestalten: Essays.* Frankfurt: Insel Verlag, 1974. 341–60.

Alexander, Franz G. and Sheldon T. Selesnick. *The History of Psychiatry: An Evolution of Psychiatric Thought and Practice from Prehistoric Times to the Present.* New York: Columbia UP, 1966.

Apter, T. E. *Fantasy Literature: An Approach to Reality.* Bloomington: Indiana UP, 1982.

Asche, Susanne. *Die Liebe, der Tod und das Ich im Spiegel der Kunst.* Königstein: Verlag Anton Hain, 1985.

Auhuber, Friedhelm. *In einem fernen dunklen Spiegel: E.T.A. Hoffmanns Poetisierung der Medizin.* Opladen: Westdeutscher Verlag, 1986.

Behrmann, Alfred. "Zur Poetik des Kunstmärchens. Eine Strukturanalyse der 'Königsbraut' von E.T.A. Hoffmann." *Erzählforschung* 3 (1978): 107–34.

Beardsley, Christa-Maria. *E.T.A. Hoffmanns Tierfiguren.* Bonn: Bouvier Verlag, 1985.

Becker, Allienne Rimer. "*The Fantastic in the Fiction of Hoffmann and Hawthorne.*" Diss. Pennsylvania State U. 1985.

Bellemin-Noël, Jean. "Notes sur le fantastique (Textes de Théophile Gautier)." *Littérature* 8 (1972): 3–23.

Bergström, Stefan. "Dark Mirrors: Fantastic Elements in E.T.A. Hoffmann's 'Die Serapionsbrüder.'" Diss. U of Kansas. 1996.

_____. "A Light-hearted Ghost Story: Supernatural Elements in E.T.A. Hoffmann's "Ein Fragment aus dem Leben dreier Freunde." *Journal of the Midlands Conference on Language & Literature* VII (1994): 6-11.

Böhme, Hartmut. "Romantische Adoleszenzkrisen: Zur Psychodynamik der Venuskult-Novellen von Tieck, Eichendorff und E. T. A. Hoffmann." *Text & Kontext* 10 (1981): 133-76.

Booth, Wayne C. *The Rhetoric of Fiction.* Chicago: Chicago UP, 1983.

Boss, Bettina. "*Die Rolle des Erzählers bei E.T.A. Hoffmanns.*" Diss. U of New South Wales, 1978.

Bourodimus, Lambro. "Todorovische Kategorien des Phantastischen, Wunderbaren und Unheimlichen in Christoph Martin Wielands 'Die Abenteuer des Don Sylvio von Rosalva' und 'Das Hexameron von Rosenhain'." Diss. U. of Kansas, 1996.

Bravo-Villasanta, Carmen. *El alucinante Mundo de E.T.A. Hoffmann.* Madrid: Nostromo, 1973.

Breuillac, Marcel. "Hoffmann en France." *Revue d'histoire littéraire de la France* 13 (1906): 427–57.

Brinkmann, Richard. Ed. *Romantik in Deutschland, ein interdisziplinares Symposium: Sonderband der Deutschen Vierteljahrschrift für Literaturwissenschaft und Geistesgeschichte.* Stuttgart: Metzler Verlag, 1978.

Brooke-Rose, Christine. *A Rhetoric of the Unreal: Studies in Narrative and Structure, Especially of the Fantastic.* Cambridge: Cambridge UP, 1981.

Bruning, Peter. "E.T.A. Hoffmann and the Philistine," *The German Quarterly* 28 (1955): 111–21.

Callois, Roger. *Anthologie du fantastique.* Paris: Gallimard, 1966.

_____. *Images, Images....* Paris: José Corti, 1966.

Casper, Bernhard. "Der historische Besen oder über die Geschichtsauffassung in E.T.A. Hoffmanns 'Serapionsbrüdern' und in der katolischen Tübinger Schule" in *Romantik in Deutschland, ein interdisziplinares Symposium: Sonderband der Deuschen Vierteljahrschrift für Literaturwissenschaft und Geistesgeschichte.* Ed. Richard Brinkmann. Stuttgart: Metzler Verlag, 1978. 490–501.

Castex, Pierre-Georges. *Le Conte fantastique en France de Nodier à Maupassant.* Paris: Corti, 1962.

Cerny, Johann. "Jacques Cazotte und E.T.A. Hoffmann." *Euphorion* 15 (1980): 140–44.

Conrad, Horst. *Die literarische Angst: Das Schreckliche in Schauerromantik und Detektivgeschichte.* Düsseldorf: Bertelsmann Universitätsverlag, 1974.

Cramer, Thomas. *Das Groteske bei E.T.A. Hoffmann.* München: Wilhelm Fink Verlag, 1970.

Crisman, William. "E. T. A. Hoffmann's 'Einsiedler Serapion' and 'Rat Krespel' as Models of Reading." *Journal of English and Germanic Philology* 81 (1986): 50-69.

Daemmrich, Horst."Zu E.T.A. Hoffmanns Bestimmung ästhetischer Fragen." *Weimarer Beiträge* 14 (1968): 640–63.

_____. "Wirklichkeit als Form: ein Aspekt Hoffmannscher Erzählkunst." *Colloqia Germanica* 4 (1970): 36–45.

_____. *The Shattered Self: E.T.A. Hoffmann's Tragic Vision.* Detroit: Wayne UP, 1973.

_____. *Themen und Motive in der Literatur. Ein Handbuch.* 2nd Ed. Tübingen: Francke, 1995.

Dattenberger, Simone. *Kommunikationsstrukturen im poetischen Werk E.T.A. Hoffmanns.* Frankfurt: Peter Lang, 1986.

de Loecker, Armand. *Zwischen Atlantis und Frankfurt: Märchendichtung und goldenes Zeitalter bei E.T.A. Hoffmann.* Frankfurt/Main and Bern: Peter Lang Verlag, 1983.

Detering, Klaus. "Der Zusammenhang der Dinge: Zum Phänomen der Integration in Hoffmanns Werk." *Mitteilungen der E.T.A. Hoffmann-Gesellschaft-Bamberg* 25 (1979): 46–50.

Diebitz, Stefan. "Übersehen und verkannt: Hoffmanns serapiontische Erzählung 'Der Zusammenhang der Dinge." *Mitteilungen der E.T.A. Hoffmann-Gesellschaft -Bamberg* 33 (1987): 50-65.

Dreike, Beate M. "Die Serapions-Brüder und der Pyramidendoktor: Marginalien zu E. T. A. Hoffmanns Kritik an der zeitgenössischen Therapeutik." *Mitteilungen der E.T.A. Hoffmann-Gesellschaft-Bamberg* 36 (1990): 15-23.

Egli, Gustav. *E.T.A. Hoffmann: Ewigkeit und Endlichkeit in seinem Werk.* Zürich: Orell Füssli, 1927.

Eilert, Heide. *Theater in der Erzählkunst. Eine Studie zum Werk E.T.A. Hoffmanns.* Tübingen: Max Niemeyer Verlag, 1977.

Ellis, John M. E.T.A. Hoffmann's "Fräulein von Scuderi." *Modern Language Notes* 64 (1969): 340–50.

_____. *Narration in the German Novelle: Theory and Interpretation.* Cambridge: Cambridge UP, 1974.

_____. "Über einige scheinbare Widersprüche in Hoffmanns Erzählungen." *Mitteilungen der E.T.A. Hoffmann-Gesellschaft-Bamberg* 29 (1983): 31-35.

Elardo, Ronald J. "E.T.A. Hoffmann's 'Nußknacker und Mausekönig.' The Mouse-Queen in the Tragedy of the Hero." in *Germanic Review* 55 (1980): 1–8.

Elardo, Ronald J. "The Maw as Infernal Medium in 'Ritter Gluck' and 'Die Bergwerke zu Falun.'" *New German Studies* 9 (1981): 29–49.

Elling, Barbara. *Leseintegration im Werk E.T.A. Hoffmanns.* Stuttgart: Verlag Paul Haupt, 1973.

Eminescu, Roxanne. "Le Fantastique." *Traveaux de linguistique et de littérature* 11, (1973): 203–213.

Ettelt, Wilhelm. *E.T.A. Hoffmann. Der Künstler und der Mensch.* Würzburg: Verlag Königshausen und Neumann, 1981.

Feldges, Brigitte and Ulrich Stadler. *E.T.A. Hoffmann. Epoche - Werk - Wirkung.* München: C.H. Beck, 1986.

Finlay, Carolyn Roberts. "The 'Miner of Falun' as Operatic Motif." *Mosaic: A Journal for the Interdisciplinary Study of Literature* 15 (1982): 47-56.

Finné, Jacques. *La Littérature fantastique.* Bruxelles: Université de Bruxelles, 1980.

Fischer, Jens Malte. "Deutschsprachige Phantastik zwischen Décadence und Faschismus." *Phaicon* 3. Frankfurt: Suhrkamp, 1978.

Freud, Sigmund. "Das Unheimliche," *Gesammelte Werke* 12. London: Imago, 1947.

Freund, Winfried. "Von der Aggression zur Angst." *Phaicon* 3. Ed. Rein Zondergeld. Frankfurt: Suhrkamp, 1978.

_____. *Die deutsche Kriminalnovelle von Schiller bis Hauptmann*. Paderborn: Ferdinand Schöningh, 1980.

_____. ed. *Phantastische Geschichten*. Stuttgart: Reclam, 1979.

Frisch, Shelley L. "Poetics of the Uncanny: E. T. A. Hoffmann's 'Sandman.'" (Sel. Essays from 1st Internat. Conf. on Fantastic in Lit. & Film). Intro. Eric S. Rabin, ed., Robert A.Collins and Howard D. Pearce. *The Scope of the Fantastic: Theory, Technique, Major Authors*. Westport: Greenwood, 1985.

Fühmann, Franz. *Fräulein Veronika Paulmann aus der Pirnaer Vorstadt oder Etwas über das Schauerliche bei E.T.A. Hoffmann*. Hamburg: Hoffmann und Campe, 1980.

Garlington, Aubry. "E.T.A. Hoffmann's 'Der Dichter und der Komponist' and the Creation of the Germanic Romantic Opera." *The Musical Quaterly* 65 (1979): 26–47.

Gendolla, Ludwig. *Die lebende Maschinen: Zur Geschichte der Maschinenmenschen bei Jean Paul, E.T.A. Hoffmann und Villiers de L'Isle Adam*. N.P. 1980.

Gillespie, Gerald. "The Romantic Discourse of Detection in Nineteenth-Century Fiction." *Fiction, narratologie, texte, genre: Actes du Symposium de l'Association Internationale de Litterature Comparee XIeme Congres International (Paris, août 1985)/Proceedings of the International Comparative Literature Association, XIth International Congress (Paris, August 1985)*, II. Ed. Jean Bessière. New York: Peter Lang, 1989.

Gorski, Gisela. *E.T.A. Hoffmanns 'Das Fräulein von Scuderi.'* Stuttgart: Akademischer Verlag Hans-Dieter Heinz, 1980.

_____. "Das Fräulein von Scuderi als Dektektivgeschichte." *Mitteilungen der E.T.A. Hoffmann-Gesellschaft-Bamberg* 27 (1981): 1–15.

Günzel, Klaus. *E.T.A. Hoffmann*. Berlin: Claasen Verlag, 1979.

Harich, Walther. *E.T.A. Hoffmann: Das Leben eines Künstlers*. Berlin: Erich Reiß, 1923.

Haase, Frank. "Eine Marginalie zu E.T.A. Hoffmanns Novelle 'Rat Krespel.'" *Mitteilungen der E.T.A. Hoffmann-Gesellschaft-Bamberg* 31 (1985): 15–17.

Harnischfeger, Johannes. *Die Hieroglyphen der inneren Welt. Romantikkritik bei E.T.A. Hoffmann*. Opladen: Westdeutscher Verlag, 1988.

Hartung, Günter. "Anatomie des Sandmanns." *Weimarer Beiträge* 23 (1977): 45–65.

Hasselberg, Felix. "Der Ästhetiker im schwarzen Rock: Zur Erklärung einer dunklen Stelle in Hoffmanns 'Brautwahl.'" *Berlinische Blätter für Geschichte und Heimatkunde* 3 (1936): 1–2.

Hayes, Charles. "Phantasie und Wirklichkeit im Werke E.T.A. Hoffmanns, mit einer Interpretation der Erzählung 'Der Sandmann.'" *Ideologiekritische Studien zur Literatur.* Frankfurt: Athenaeum, 1972.

Heilbronn, Ernst. "E.T.A. Hoffmann und das Automat." *Das literarische Echo* 28 (1925): 72–75.

Heinisch, Klaus J. "E.T.A. Hoffmann: 'Die Bergwerke zu Falun.'" *Deutsche Romantik: Interpretationen.* Paderborn: Ferdinand Schöningh, 1966. 134–153.

Heinritz, Reinhard. "Philologie der Rede-Erfindungen: Die Diskursanalyse im Spiegel ihrer E. T. A.-Hoffmann-Texte." *Mitteilungen der E.T.A. Hoffmann -Gesellschaft-Bamberg* 35 (1989): 49-57.

Heinz, Günter. "Mechanik und Phantasie. Zu E.T.A. Hoffmanns Märchen 'Nußknacker und Mausekönig.'" *Literatur in Wissenschaft und Unterricht* 7 (1974): 1–15.

Helmke, Ulrich. *E.T.A. Hoffmann.* Kassel: Georg Wenderoth Verlag, 1975.

Hemmerich, Gerd. "Verteidigung des Signor Formica: Zu E.T.A. Hoffmanns Novelle." *Jahrbuch der Jean Paul-Gesellschaft* 17 (1982): 113–28.

Hewett-Thayer, Harvey. *Hoffmann: Author of the Tales.* Princeton: Princeton UP, 1948.

Hillmann, Heinz. *Bildlichkeit der deutschen Romantik.* Frankfurt am Main: Athenäum, 1971.

Himmel, Hellmuth. "Schuld und Sühne der Scuderi." *Mitteilungen der E.T.A. Hoffmann-Gesellschaft* 7 (1960): 1–15.

Hohoff, Ulrich. *E.T.A. Hoffmann: Der Sandmann.* Berlin: Walter de Gruyter, 1988.

Holbeche, Yvonne Jill. *Optical Motifs in the Works of E.T.A. Hoffmann.* Göppingen: Verlag Alfred Kümmerle, 1975.

_____. "The Relationship of the Artist to Power: E.T.A. Hoffmann's 'Das Fräulein von Scuderi,'" *Seminar* 16 (1981): 1–11.

Holländer, Barbara. "Augenblicke der Verwandlung in E.T.A. Hoffmanns Märchen 'Der goldene Topf'". *Augenblick und Zeitpunkt. Studien zur Zeitstruktur und Zeitmetaphorik in Kunst und Wissenschaften.* Ed. Christian W. Thomsen/Hans Holländer. Darmstadt: Wissenschaftlicher Buchverlag, 1984.

Huch, Ricarda. *Die Romantik: Blütezeit, Ausbreitung und Verfall.* Tübingen: Rainer Wunderlich Verlag, 1951.

Irwin, W.R. *The Game of the Impossible: A Rhetoric of Fantasy.* Urbana: U of Illinois P, 1976.

Jacquemin, Georges. "Über das Phantastische in Literatur." *Phaicon 2.* Ed. Rein Zondergeld. Frankfurt: Insel, 1975.

Jennings, Lee B. "Hoffmann's Hauntings: Notes toward a Parapsychological Approach to Literature." *Journal of English and Germanic Philology.* 75 (1976): 559–67.

_____. "The Anatomy of Spuk in Two Tales of E. T. A. Hoffmann." *Colloquia Germanica, Internationale Zeitschrift fur Germanische Sprach- und Literaturwissenschaft* 17, (1984): 60-78.

_____. "The Downward Transcendence: Hoffmann's Bergwerke zu Falun." *Deutsche Vierteljahrsschrift für Literaturwissenschaft und Geistesgeschichte* 59. (1985): 278–89.

Kaiser, Gerhard R. *E.T.A. Hoffmann.* Stuttgart: J. B. Metzlersche Verlagsbuchhandlung, 1988.

Kamla, Thomas A. "E. T. A. Hoffmann's Vampirism Tale: Instinctual Perversion." *American Imago: A Psychoanalytic Journal for Culture, Science, and the Arts* 42. (1985): 235-53.

Kanzog, Klaus. "E.T.A. Hoffmanns Erzählung 'Fräulein von Scuderi' als Kriminalgeschichte." *Mitteilungen der E.T.A. Hoffmann-Gesellschaft-Bamberg* 11. (1964): 1–11.

Kanzog, Klaus. "Formel, Motiv, Requisit und Zeichen bei E.T.A. Hoffmann." *Romantik in Deutschland. Ein interdisziplinäres Symposium: Sonderband der Deutschen Vierteljahrschrift für Literaturwissenschaft und Geistesgeschichte.* Ed. Richard Brinkmann. Stuttgart: Metzler Verlag, 1978. 625–38.

Karoli, Christa. "E.T.A. Hoffmann und Zacharias Werner." *Mitteilungen der E.T.A. Hoffmann-Gesellschaft-Bamberg* 16 (1970): 43–61.

Kayser, Wolfgang. *Das Groteske. Seine Gestaltung in Malerei und Dichtung.* 2nd Ed. Oldenburg: Stalling, 1961.

Klein, Johannes. *Geschichte der deutschen Novelle von Goethe bis zur Gegenwart.* Wiesbaden: Steiner, 1960.

Kleßmann, Eckart. *E.T.A. Hoffmann oder die Tiefe zwischen Stern und Erde.* Stuttgart: Deutsche Verlagsanstalt, 1988.

Köhn, Lothar. *Vieldeutige Welt: Studien zur Struktur der Erzählungen E.T.A. Hoffmanns und zur Entwicklung des Werkes.* Tübingen: Max Niemeyer Verlag, 1966.

Kolke, Inge. "Aus den Gräbern zerrst Du Deine Atzung, teuflisches Weib!': Verwesung als strukturbildendes Element in E. T. A. Hoffmanns Vampirismus-Geschichte." *Mitteilungen der E.T.A. Hoffmann-Gesellschaft-Bamberg* 33 (1987): 34-49.

Korff, Hermann August. *Geist der Goethezeit.* Leipzig: Koehler und Amelang, 1964.

Krauss, Wilhelmine. *Das Doppelgängermotiv in der Romantik: Studien zum romantischen Idealismus.* Berlin: Ebering, 1930.

Kropf, David Glenn. "*Authorship and Literary Subversions in the Romantic Period: Pushkin, Scott, Hoffmann.*" Diss. Stanford U. 1991.

Kuttner, Margot. *Die Gestaltung des Individualitätsproblem bei E.T.A. Hoffmann.* Diss. U. Hamburg, 1935. Düsseldorf: Dissertationsverlag G.H. Noltke, 1936.

Lawson, Ursula. "Pathological Time in E.T.A. Hoffmann's 'Der Sandmann'" *Monatshefte* LX (1968): 51–61.

Lehmann, Jakob, ed. *Deutsche Novellen von Goethe bis Walser.* Königstein: Scriptor, 1980.

Lem, Stanislaw. "Todorov's Fantastic Theory of Literature: Suggestions on how to define and analyze Fantastic Fiction." *Science Fiction Studies* 1 (1974): 227–37.

Liedke-Konow, Petra Ursula. "*E. T. A. Hoffmanns 'Serapions-Brüder': Eine Analyse Unter zeichen- und kommunikationstheoretischen Aspekten.*" Diss. UCLA, Los Angeles, 1991.

Lindken, Hans-Ulrich. *E.T.A. Hoffmann: "Das Fräulein von Scuderi." Erläuterungen und Dokumente.* Stuttgart: Philip Reclam, 1978.

Loepp, Frida. "*Über E.T.A. Hoffmann's 'Kampf der Sänger.'*" Diss. Marburg: 1925.

von Maasen, Carl Georg. "Hoffmanns Erzählung die Fermate und Hummels Gemälde Die Gesellschaft in einer italienischen Lokanda.*" Der grundgeschaute Antiquarius* 2 (1923): 68–71.

Magris, Claudio. *Die andere Vernunft: E.T.A. Hoffmann.* Königstein: Verlag Anton Hain, 1980.

von Matt, Peter. *Die Augen der Automaten: E.T.A. Hoffmanns Imaginationslehre als Prinzip seiner Erzählkunst.* Tübingen: Max Niemeyer, 1971.

_____. "Die gemalte Geliebte." *Germanisch-Romanische Monatschrift* 21 (1971): 395–412.

Mayer, Hans. "Die Wirklichkeit E.T.A. Hoffmanns" in *Von Lessing bis Thomas Mann: Wandlungen der bürgerlichen Literatur in Deutschland*. Pfullingen: Verlag Günther Neske, 1959. 198–246.

McGlathery, James M. "Der Himmel hängt ihm voller Geigen: E.T.A. Hoffmann's 'Rat Krespel,' 'Die Fermate' and 'Der Baron von B.'" *German Quarterly* 51 (1978): 135–49.

_____. *Mysticism and Sexuality: E.T.A. Hoffmann*. Las Vegas: Peter Lang, 1981.

_____. *E.T.A Hoffmann*. Twayne's World Authors Series 868. New York: Twayne, 1997.

Meyer-Krentler, Eckhardt. "'Die verkaufte Braut': Juristische und literarische Wirklichkeitssicht im 18. und frühen 19. Jahrhundert." *Lessing Yearbook/Jahrbuch* 16 (1984): 95-123.

Miller, Norbert. "E.T.A. Hoffmann und die Musik." *Zu E.T.A. Hoffmann*. Ed. Steven Paul Scher. Stuttgart: Klett Verlag, 1981.

Mollenauer, Robert. "The Three Periods of E.T.A. Hoffmann's Romanticism: An Attempt at a Definition." *Studies in Romanticism* 2 (1963): 213–43.

Momberger, Manfred. *Sonne und Punsch: Die Dissemination des romantischenKunstbegriffs bei E.T.A. Hoffmann*. München: Wilhelm Fink Verlag, 1986.

Motekat, Helmut. "Vom sehen und Erkennen bei E.T.A. Hoffmann." *Mitteilungen der E.T.A. Hoffmann-Gesellschaft* 19 (1973): 17–27.

Mühlher, Robert. "Leitmotiv und dialektischer Mythos in E.T.A. Hoffmanns Märchen 'Der goldene Topf.'" *Mitteilungen der E.T.A. Hoffmann-Gesellschaft* 1 (1940): 65–96.

_____. "E.T.A. Hoffmann. Beiträge zu einer Motiv-Interpretation." *Litteraturwissenschaftliches Jahrbuch der Goethe-Gesellschaft* 4 (1963): 55–72.

_____. *Deutsche Dichter der Klassik und der Romantik*. Wien: Wilhelm Braumüller, 1976.

Müller, Dieter. "Zeit der Automate: Zum Automatenproblem bei Hoffmann." *Mitteilungen der E.T.A. Hoffmann-Gesellschaft* 12 (1966): 1–8.

von Müller, Hans. *Gesammelte Aufsätze über E.T.A. Hoffmann*. Hildesheim: Verlag Dr. H.A. Gerstenberg, 1974.

Müller, Helmut. *Untersuchungen zum Problem der Formelhaftigkeit bei E.T.A. Hoffmann*. Bern: Verlag Paul Haupt, 1964.

136

Negus, Kenneth. "E.T.A. Hoffmann's 'Der goldene Topf': Its Romantic Myth." *Germanic Review* 32 (1959): 262–275.

_____. *E.T.A. Hoffmann's Other World.* Philadelphia: U of Pennsylvania P, 1965.

Nehring, Wolfgang. "E.T.A. Hoffmanns Erzählwerk: Ein Modell und seine Variationen." *Zeitschrift für deutsche Philologie* 95 (1976): 3–24.

Neubauer, John. "The Mines of Falun: Temporal Fortunes of a Romantic Myth." *Studies in Romanticism* 19 (1980): 475–95.

Nipperdey, Otto. *"Wahnsinnsfiguren bei E.T.A. Hoffmann."* Diss. Köln: 1957.

Ochsner, Karl. *E.T.A. Hoffmann als Dichter des Unbewußten.* Frauenfeld: Huber & Co., 1936.

Olbrich, Karl. "E.T.A. Hoffmann und die deutsche Volksglaube." *E.T.A. Hoffmann.* Ed. Helmut Prang. Darmstadt: Wissenschaftliche Buchgesellschaft, 1976. 56–88.

Ostrowski, W. "The Fantastic and the Realistic in Literature, Suggestions on how to define and analyze fantastic fiction." *Zagadnienia rodzajow literackich* 9 (1966): 54–71.

Paretski, Jonathan M. "Isaac Bashevis Singer's Short Fiction and the Function of the Fantastic." Diss. U. of Kansas, 1991.

Peters, Diana Stone. "The Dream as Bridge in the Works of E.T.A. Hoffmann." *Oxford German Studies* 8 (1973): 60–85.

_____."E.T.A. Hoffmann: The Concilliatory Satirist." *Monatshefte* 66 (1974): 55–73.

Pfotenhauer, Helmut. "Exotische und esoterische Poetik in E.T.A. Hoffmanns Erzählungen." *Jahrbuch der Jean-Paul-Gesellschaft* 17 (1982): 129–44.

Pikulik, Lothar. *E.T.A. Hoffmann als Erzähler: Ein Kommentar zu den "Serapionsbrüdern."* Göttingen: Vandenhoeck & Ruprecht, 1987.

_____. "Das Wunderliche bei E.T.A. Hoffmann: Zum romantischen Ungenügen an der Normalität." *Euphorion* 69 (1975): 294–319.

Pistor, Carl. "Eine Marginalie zu E. T. A. Hoffmanns Novelle 'Rat Krespel.'" *Mitteilungen der E.T.A. Hoffmann-Gesellschaft-Bamberg* 31 (1985): 15-17.

Pix, Günther. "Der Variationskünstler E. T. A. Hoffmann und seine Erzählung 'Der Artushof.'" *Mitteilungen der E.T.A. Hoffmann-Gesellschaft-Bamberg* 35 (1989): 5-20.

von Planta, Urs Oland. *E.T.A. Hoffmann's Märchen "Das Fremde Kind."* Bern: Francke Verlag, 1958.

Pniower, Otto. "E.T.A. Hoffmanns Erzählung 'Aus dem Leben eines bekannten Mannes.'" *Euphorion* 14 (1907): 714–17.

Post, Klaus D. "Kriminalgeschichte als Heilsgeschichte: Zu E.T.A. Hoffmanns Erzählung 'Das Fräulein von Scuderi.'" *Zeitschrift für deutsche Philologie* 95 (1976): 132–56.

Prang, Helmut, ed. *E.T.A. Hoffmann: Wege der Forschung* Darmstadt: Wissenschaftliche Buchgesellschaft, 1970.

Prawer, S.S. "E.T.A. Hoffmann's uncanny Guest: A Reading of 'Der Sandmann,'" *German Life and Letters* 18, (1964–65):

Preisedanz, Wolfgang. "Eines matt geschiliffenen Spiegels dunkler Widerschein: E.T.A. Hoffmanns Erzählkunst" in *Zu E.T.A. Hoffmann*. Stuttgart: 1981. 40–54.

Psaar, Werner. "Ernst Theodor Amadeus Hoffmann: 'Das Fräulein von Scuderi'" *Deutsche Novellen von Goethe bis Walser*. Ed. Jakob Lehmann. Königstein: Scriptor, 1980.

Rabkin, Eric S. *The Fantastic in Literature*. Princeton: Princeton UP, 1976.

Retinger, Joseph. *Le Conte fantastique dans le romantisme français*. Paris: 1909; rpt. Genève: Sklatin Reprints, 1973.

Ricci, Jean. *E.T.A. Hoffmann. L'homme et l'œvre*. Paris: Corti, 1947.

_____. "Le Fantastique dans l'œuvres d'E.T.A. Hoffmann." *Études Germaniques* 6 (1951): 100–16.

Riemer, Elke. *E.T.A. Hoffmann und seine Illustratoren*. Hildesheim: Verlag Dr. H.A. Gerstenberg, 1976.

Rippley, La Vern. "The House as Metaphor in E.T.A. Hoffmann's 'Rat Krespel.'" *Papers on Language and Literature* 7 (1971): 52–60.

Rockenbach, Nickolaus. *"Bauformen romantischer Kunstmärchen Eine Studie zur epischen Integration des Wunderbaren bei E.T.A. Hoffmann."* Diss. Bonn: 1957.

Roters, Eberhard. *E.T.A. Hoffmann*. Berlin: Stapp Verlag, n.d.

Roy, Claude. "Psychologie du fantastique." *Les Temps modernes* 166–8 (1960): 1393–1416.

Safranski, Rüdiger. *E.T.A. Hoffmann*. München: Carl Hanser Verlag, 1984.

Sahlin, Johanna., ed. *Selected Letters of E.T.A. Hoffmann*. Chicago: U of Chicago P, 1977.

138

Schaukal, Richard von. *E.T.A. Hoffmann: Sein Werk aus seinem Leben*. Zürich: Amalthea-Bücherei, 1923.

Schenk, Ernst von. *E.T.A. Hoffmann: Ein Kampf um das Bild des Menschen*. Berlin: Verlag die Runde, 1939.

Scher, Steven Paul. *Interpretationen zu E.T.A. Hoffmann*. Stuttgart: Ernst Klett Verlag, 1981.

Schmitz-Emans, Monika. "Der durchbrochene Rahmen: Überlegungen zu einem Strukturmodell des Phantastischen bei E. T. A. Hoffmann." *Mitteilungen der E.T.A. Hoffmann-Gesellschaft-Bamberg* 32 (1986): 74-88.

Schnapp, Friedrich. "Der Seraphinerorden und die Serapionsbrüder." *Literaturwissenschaftliches Jahrbuch* 3 (1962): 1–112.

———. "Die Heimat des fremden Kindes." *Mitteilungen der E.T.A. Hoffmann-Gesellschaft-Bamberg* 21 (1975): 38–41.

Schnapp, Friedrich (Ed.). *E.T.A. Hoffmann in Aufzeichnungen seiner Freunde und Bekannten*. München: Winkler Verlag, 1974.

Schneider, Karl Ludwig. "Künstlerliebe und Philistertum im Werk E.T.A. Hoffmanns." *Die Deutsche Romantik*. Ed. Hans Steffen. Göttingen: Vandenhoeck & Ruprecht, 1978. 200–18.

Schneider, Marcel. *La Littérature fantastique*. Paris: Fayard, 1964.

Schneider, Peter. "Verbrechen, Künstlertum und Wahnsinn: Untersuchungen zur Figur des Cardillac in E. T. A. Hoffmanns 'Das Fräulein von Scuderi.'" *Mitteilungen der E.T.A. Hoffmann-Gesellschaft-Bamberg* 26 (1980): 34-50.

Schubert, Gotthilf, Heinrich. *Ansichten von der Nachtseite der Naturwissenschaft*. Dresden 1808; Nachdruck, Darmstadt: Wissenschaftliche Buchgesellschaft, 1967.

Schumacher, Hans. *Narziß an der Quelle: Das romantische Kunstmärchen*. Wiesbaden: Athenaion, 1977.

Schumm, Siegfried. *Einsicht und Darstellung*. Göppingen: Verlag Alfed Kümmerle, 1974.

Scott, Walther. "On the Supernatural in Ficticious Composition; and particularly on the Works of Ernest Theodore William Hoffmann." *The Foreign Quarterly Review*. (1827): 61–98.

Schweitzer, Christopher F. "Bild, Struktur und Bedeutung: E.T.A. Hoffmanns 'Die Fermate.'" *Mitteilungen der E.T.A. Hoffmann-gesellschaft-Bamberg* 19 (1973): 49–51.

Segebrecht, Wulf. *Autobiographie und Dichtung: Eine Studie zum Werk E.T.A. Hoffmanns*. Stuttgart: J.B. Metzlersche Verlagsbuchhandlung, 1967.

Siebers, Tobin. *The Romantic Fantastic*. Ithaca: Cornell UP, 1984.

_____. "'Whose Hideous Voice Is This?' The Reading Unconscious in Freud and Hoffmann." *New Orleans Review* 15:3 (1988): 80-87.

Siganos, André. "Sur Hoffmann et George Sand: 'L'Histoire du véritable Gribouille' et 'L'Enfant étranger." *Revue de Litterature Comparée* 56 (1982): 92-95.

Sommer, Paul. *Erläuterungen zu E.T.A. Hoffmanns 'Meister Martin der Küfer und seine Gesellen.'* Leipzig: König, 1930.

Sommerhage, Claus. "Hoffmanns Erzähler. Über Poetik und Psychologie in E.T.A. Hoffmanns Nachstück 'Der Sandmann.'" *Zeitschrift für deutsche Philologie* 106 (1985): 513–34.

Steffen, Hans, ed. *Die Deutsche Romantik*. Göttingen: Vandenhoeck & Ruprecht, 1978.

Stegman, Inge. "Die Wirklichkeit des Traumes bei E.T.A. Hoffmann" *Zeitschrift für deutsche Philologie* 95 (1976): 64–92.

Stiffler, Muriel W. *The German Ghost Story as Genre*. New York: Peter Lang, 1993.

Strohschneider-Kohrs, *Ingrid. Die romantische Ironie in Theorie und Gestalt*. 2nd Ed. Tübingen: Niemeyer, 1977

Sucher, Paul. *Les Sources du merveilleux chez E.T.A. Hoffmann*. Paris: Felix Alcan, 1912.

Swann, William. *"The Technique of Softening: E.T.A. Hoffmann's Presentation of the Fantastic."* Diss. Yale, 1971.

Taylor, Ronald. *Hoffmann*. London: Bowes & Bowes, 1963.

Tauber, Serge. *"Die Bedeutung der Künstlerischen Menschenfigur im Werke E.T.A. Hoffmanns."* Diss. Innsbruck: 1959.

Thalmann, Marianne. "E.T.A. Hoffmanns 'Fräulein von Scuderi.'" *Monatshefte für Deutschunterricht* 41 (1949): 107–16.

Toggenburger, Hans. *Die späten Almanach-Erzählungen E.T.A. Hoffmanns*. Bern/Frankfurt/New York: Peter Lang, 1983.

Todorov, Tzvetan. *Introduction à la littérature fantastique*. Paris: Éditions du Seuil, 1970.

Tretter, Friedrich Giselher. *"Die Frage nach der Wirklichkeit bei E.T.A. Hoffmann."* Diss. München: 1961.

Vax, Louis. "L'Art de faire peur." *Critique* 12 (1959): 934–42 and 1026–48.

_____. *Séduction de l'étrange.* Paris: Presses Universitaires de France, 1965.

Vietta, Silvio. "Das Automatenmotiv und die Technik der Motivschichtung im Erzählwerk E.T.A. Hoffmanns." *Mitteilungen der E.T.A. Hoffmann-Gesellschaft-Bamberg* 30 (1984): 25–33.

Vitt-Maucher, Gisela. "Hoffmanns 'Rat Krespel' und der Schlafrock Gottes." *Monatshefte* 64 (1972): 51–57.

_____. "Die wunderliche wunderbare Welt E.T.A. Hoffmanns." *Journal of English and Germanic Philology* 75 (1976): 515–30.

_____. "E. T. A. Hoffmanns 'Die Königsbraut': Ein nach der Natur entworfenes Märchen." *Mitteilungen der E.T.A. Hoffmann-Gesellschaft-Bamberg* 30 (1984): 42-58.

_____. *E.T.A. Hoffmanns Märchenschaffen. Kaleidoskop der Verfremdung in seinen sieben Märchen.* Chapel Hill: The U of North Carolina P, 1989.

Voerster, Jürgen. *160 Jahre E.T.A. Hoffmann-Forschung.* Stuttgart: Verlag Fritz Eggert, 1967.

Waggoner, Dianna. *The Hills of Faraway: A Guide to Fantasy.* New York: Atheneum, 1978.

Wanduszka, Maria Luisa. *La Casa del Consiliere Krespel. Figure de identita nella letteratura tedesca.* Bologna: Cooperativa Libraria Universitaria Editrice, 1985.

Wawrzyn, Lienhard. *Der Automaten-Mensch. E.T.A. Hoffmanns Erzählung vom Sandmann.* Berlin: Klaus Wagenbach, 1976.

Weinholz, Gerhard. *E.T.A. Hoffmann. Dichter—Psychologe—Jurist.* Essen: Verlag die Blaue Eule, 1991.

_____. *E.T.A. Hoffmanns Erzählung "Die Automate".* Essen: Verlag die Blaue Eule, 1991.

Wellek, René. *Confrontations: Studies in the Intellectual and Literary Relations between Germany, England and the United States during the Nineteenth Century.* Princeton: Princeton UP, 1965.

Wellenberger, Georg. *Der Unernst des Unendlichen: Die Poetologie der Romantik und ihre Umsetzung durch E.T.A. Hoffmann.* Marburg: Hitzeroth, 1986.

Werner, Hans-Georg. *E.T.A. Hoffmann.* Berlin: Aufbau-Verlag, 1971.

Werner, Johannes. "Was treibt Cardillac? Ein Goldschmied auf Abwegen." *Wirkendes Wort: Deutsche Sprache und Literatur in Forschung und Lehre* 40 (1990): 32-38.

von Wiese, Benno. "E.T.A. Hoffmann: Rat Krespel." *Die deutsche Novelle von Goethe bis Kafka*. Düsseldorf: 1962.

Wight, Doris T. "Masochism, Mourning, Melancholia: A Freudian Interpretation of E. T. A. Hoffmann's Tale 'The Mines of Falun.'" *Germanic Notes* 21 (1990): 49-55.

Willimczik, Kurt. *E.T.A. Hoffmann: Die drei Reiche seiner Gestaltenwelt*. Diss. Berlin: Neue deutsche Forschungen, Junker und Dünnhaupt, 1939.

Winter, Ilse. *Untersuchungen zum serapiontischen Prinzip E.T.A. Hoffmanns*. The Hague: Mouton & Co., 1976.

Wittkop-Ménardeau, Gabrielle. *E.T.A. Hoffmann in Selbstzeugnissen und Bilddokumenten*. Reineck bei Hamburg: Rowolth, 1966.

Wittkowski, Wolfgang. "E.T.A. Hoffmanns musikalische Musikerdichtungen 'Ritter Gluck,' 'Don Juan,' 'Rat Krespel.'" *Aurora* 38 (1978): 54–74.

Wolfe, Gary K. "Symbolic Fantasy." *Genre* 8 (1975): 194–209.

Wöllner, Günter. *E.T.A. Hoffmann und Franz Kafka. Von der fortgeführten Metapher zum sinnlichen Paradox*. Bern: Verlag Paul Haupt, 1971.

Wright, Elisabeth. *E.T.A. Hoffmann and The Rhetoric of Terror*. London: Institute of Germanic Studies, 1978.

Wucherpfennig. "Die alte Dame und die Kriminalgeschichte der Seele, Überlegungen zu E.T.A. Hoffmanns 'Fräulein von Scuderi.'" *Studia Germanica Gandensia* 8 (1986): 200–204.

Zgorzelski, Andrzej. "Is Science Fiction a Genre of Fantastic Literature?" *Science Fiction Studies* 6 (1979): 296–303.

Ziegler, Vickie L. *Bending the Frame in the German Cyclical Narrative. Achim von Arnim's "Der Wintergarten" & E.T.A. Hoffmann's "Die Serapionsbrüder."* Washington: The Catholic U of America P, 1991.

Ziolkowski, Theodore. "Der Karfunkelstein." *Euphorion* 55 (1961): 297–326.

_____. *German Romanticism and its Institutions*. Princeton: Princeton UP, 1990.

Zondergeld, Rein. ed. *Phaicon* 1–3. 3 vols. Frankfurt: Suhrkamp, 1975–8.

_____. "Zwei Versuche der Befreiung." *Phaicon* 2, Ed. Rein Zondergeld, Frankfurt: Suhrkamp, 1975.

Studies on Themes and Motifs in Literature

The series is designed to advance the publication of research pertaining to themes and motifs in literature. The studies cover cross-cultural patterns as well as the entire range of national literatures. They trace the development and use of themes and motifs over extended periods, elucidate the significance of specific themes or motifs for the formation of period styles, and analyze the unique structural function of themes and motifs. By examining themes or motifs in the work of an author or period, the studies point to the impulses authors received from literary tradition, the choices made, and the creative transformation of the cultural heritage. The series will include publications of colloquia and theoretical studies that contribute to a greater understanding of literature.

For additional information about this series or for the submission of manuscripts, please contact:

Peter Lang Publishing
Acquisitions Dept.
516 N. Charles St., 2nd Floor
Baltimore, MD 21201

To order other books in this series, please contact our Customer Service Department:

800-770-LANG (within the U.S.)
212-647-7706 (outside the U.S.)
212-647-7707 FAX

Or browse online by series at:

www.peterlang.com